THE LIBERATION CHRISTOLOGIES OF LEONARDO BOFF AND JON SOBRINO

Latin American Contributions to Contemporary Christology

Donald E. Waltermire
St. John Center, Inc.

UNIVERSITY
PRESS OF
AMERICA

Lanham • New York • London

Copyright © 1994 by
University Press of America®, Inc.
4720 Boston Way
Lanham, Maryland 20706

3 Henrietta Street
London WC2E 8LU England

Library of Congress Cataloging-in-Publication Data

Waltermire, Donald E.
The liberation christologies of Leonardo Boff and Jon Sobrino :
Latin American contributions to contemporary christology /
Donald E. Waltermire.
p.   cm.
Includes bibliographical references and index.
1. Jesus Christ—History of doctrines—20th century.   2. Liberation
theology.   3. Boff, Leonardo.   4. Sobrino, Jon.   I. Title.
BT198.W36   1993   232'.092'28—dc20   92–40305 CIP

ISBN 0–8191–9018–7 (alk. paper)

TABLE OF CONTENTS

PREFACE

This book is the result of the influence of many people on my life. I am indebted to Frank Tupper for his contention that Christology is the heart of Christian theology and is the basis of one's life and praxis. He has provided me with a way to understand theology and its relation to life, a gift that I am only beginning to appreciate. My dissertation supervisor, David L. Mueller, has influenced me in several ways. He introduced me to liberation theology via the writings of Letty M. Russell and José Míguez Bonino. His patient and critical reading of the manuscript enabled me to get a firmer grasp on my subject matter and sharpened my own critical skills. Finally, I had the opportunity to study at Yale Divinity School with Letty M. Russell. Under her tutelage I was able to immerse myself in Latin American liberation theology and feminist theology.

I owe a special degree of gratitude and appreciation to my friend, Martha J. Spiegel. She not only translated several of Boff's works that were in the original Portuguese, but she also served as a sounding board for my tentative conclusions. Without her assistance, my understanding of Boff would have been less thorough. Finally, I must acknowledge the technical assistance provided me by St. John's Center for the Homeless, which graciously allowed me to use its computer for my writing.

After my initial introduction to liberation theology, I began to delve into its christological aspects. The more I read, the more enthralled I became with "Jesus the Liberator." As I continued to read, I began to focus on works from Latin America. I eventually discovered the christological writings of Leonardo Boff and Jon Sobrino. I decided that they would be the focus of my study. As I began my research, I was taken aback by the lack of response from the theological world at large; I found that these works were all but ignored in scholarly debate. Thus, it is my intention to facilitate theological conversation concerning their works.

Methodology

The methodology to be utilized in this book is chronological, descriptive, and analytical in nature. Chronology is evident in two ways. First, chapter one will consist of a brief analysis of the modern theological roots of liberation by focusing on the Second Vatican Council and its implementation by the Second General Conference of Latin American Bishops in Medellín, Colombia, in 1968. Second, Boff's Christology, which was published first, will also be examined first.

The methodology is descriptive in that I will assess the major emphases of the Christologies of Boff and Sobrino. As much as is possible, they will be allowed to speak for themselves, letting their historical situations, presuppositions, and biases have free rein. These issues will be dealt with in chapter five. Thus, chapter two will be an exposition of Boff's christological thought and Sobrino's works will be the subject of chapter three.

The analytical aspect will be seen in chapters four and five. Chapter four will be a delineation of the individual contributions of Boff and Sobrino to the study of Christology. Then, somewhat artificially, they will be combined into one christological construction. Chapter five will consist of a critique by selected non-Latin American theologians. Pope John Paul II and the Sacred Congregation for the Doctrine of the Faith comprise the Roman Catholic response; Schubert M. Ogden is the representative of a liberal Protestant response; Clark H. Pinnock provides an Evangelical critique; and I will end the chapter with my evaluation of liberation Christology.

Delimitations

Several delimitations need to be made lest this study become too expansive. First, the ramifications of liberation Christology for the whole of systematic theology will not be fleshed out. Where appropriate, the impact of this Christology upon the understanding of any given subject matter will be discussed and evaluated. Second, the relationship of Latin American Christology to non-Latin American liberation theologies will not be examined. "Liberation theology" now has several branches: feminist, African American, African, and Asian. While this type of relationship would be a worthwhile and informative study, it is beyond the scope of this book. Third, the contributions of Latin America to contemporary Christology are derived from a dialogue between Boff, Sobrino, Wolfhart Pannenberg, and Jürgen Moltmann that I have contrived. I contend that, even though Boff and Sobrino are Roman Catholic, their major dialogue partners vis-à-vis methodology and content, are Pannenberg and Moltmann. Finally, the most telling delimitation is that I, a white North American male, am attempting to analyze and critique a Latin American Christology. Misrepresentations, misinterpretations, and missed interpretations are bound to happen; such is the nature of contextuality and cross-cultural dialogue. Should any of these occur, I alone am responsible for them and I apologize for them beforehand.

Donald E. Waltermire

Louisville, Kentucky

November 1992

Chapter 1

INTRODUCTION

Liberation theology exploded onto the international theological scene in 1973 with the English translation of Gustavo Gutiérrez's *Teología de la liberación, Perspectivas.* This theology, however, did not materialize out of thin air. This chapter will serve as an introduction to selected aspects of the modern theological roots of liberation theology. The history of Latin America has been well documented elsewhere and will not be discussed here.[1] What will be discussed are certain themes of the Second Vatican Council and their interpretation by the Second General Conference of Latin American Bishops (CELAM) in Medellín, Colombia. During the course of this conference, certain characteristics of liberation theology arose because of the unique situation in which Latin America found itself. The more foundational characteristics will be examined in order to orient the reader to liberation theology and its methodology.

The Second Vatican Council

The Second Vatican Council was concerned with the relationship of the Church to the modern world.[2] This concern led the assembled clerics to examine traditional beliefs in a new light. The whys and wherefores of an age characterized by violence were expounded and reinterpreted in light of the gospel. For the Church to make inroads into the state of affairs that exist in the twentieth century, the Council said it must be cognizant of "the broader desires of mankind."[3] These desires encompass the political, social, and economic spheres of life that serve to help or hinder the growth of dignity of individuals and of groups of people. According to the council, there seems to be a new universal belief "that the benefits of culture ought to be and actually can be extended to everyone."[4]

But in spite of this belief, "nations on the road to progress . . . . continually fall behind while very often their dependence on wealthier nations deepens more rapidly."[5] The reason for this situation is the "lordly fashion" which "foreign experts" render their assistance, that is, national self-aggrandizement. The council stated unequivocally that a state of dependence will continue unless:

> an abolition of excessive desire for profit, nationalistic pretensions, the lust for political domination, militaristic thinking and intrigues designed to spread and impose ideologies [occurs].[6]

In other words, assistance should not be rendered so as to promote the interests of the dominant nation over the interests of the receiving nation. The goal is to help the underdeveloped nation; its progress should not be coincidental.

The role that dependence and developmentalist theories play in the quest for liberation was recognized by the council.7 It realized that this type of thinking places great emphasis upon the economic and social arenas of life, causing some people to believe that liberation would be anticipated by economic and social emancipation accomplished solely through human effort. On the one hand, the council was not adverse to emphasizing the need for economic and social overhaul. By taking this stand, the council expressed its hope for "the birth of a new humanism, one in which man is defined first of all by his responsibility toward his brothers and toward history."8 Such a responsibility entails the "building up of the world." In doing so, humanity is fulfilled and transcended. By what it does, humanity can gather together its:

> humane, domestic, professional, social, and technical enterprises into one vital synthesis with religious values, under whose supreme direction all things are harmonized unto God's glory.9

On the other hand, the council was mindful of the fact that "earthly progress must be carefully distinguished from the growth of Christ's kingdom."10 The former is of concern to the latter only in as much as it can better the organizing of human society. It was the council's position that "Christ . . . gave His Church no proper mission in the political, economic, or social order. The purpose which He set before her is a religious one."11 In other words, there is only one God, one history, and one humanity. The history of salvation includes the order of creation; transcendence subsumes immanence. Active involvement in this world is important, but secondary.

Despite the fact that the council's balance between the value of worldly activity and that of religious activity has a definite tilt towards the latter, its concern for the former should be fully appreciated. The documents of the Second Vatican Council as a whole emphasize a Church of service over a Church of power. This type of Church begins with the recognition that "the joys and the hopes, the griefs and the anxieties of the men of this age, especially those who are poor or in any way afflicted . . . are [those] of the followers of Christ."12 Thus, it is the common bond of human experience that intimately connects the Church with the world; religious activity with mundane activity. Any attempt to focus solely upon the spiritual realm reveals a lack of understanding of the gospel.

The singling out of the poor and the afflicted is significant. This act should not be understood as the sanctification of some sentimental philanthropy into dogma; rather, it stems from the fact that the Church "recognizes in the poor and the suffering the likeness of her poor and suffering Founder."13 This appeal to the example of Christ has two results. First, by serving the poor and the suffering the Church is serving Christ who "by His incarnation . . . has united Himself in some fashion with every man."14 Second, by appealing to Christ who "carried out the work of redemption in poverty and under oppression," the Church acknowledges the fact that it "is called to follow the same path in communicating to men the fruits of salvation."15

This emphasis upon the poor and the suffering of the world impacts greatly the way in which the Church conducts itself in the world. The council recognized the fact that the Church needs "human resources" to fulfill its mission although it "is not set up to seek earthly glory, but to proclaim humility and self-sacrifice, even by her own example."[16] Therefore, its priests are to give the management of these resources over to competent laypeople who will use them for the upkeep of the parish and for the needy. In a similar vein, priests and their bishops are to "avoid all those things which can offend the poor in any way."[17] This action will allow the Church to become more of a servant because the clergy begins its ministry at the bottom, that is, with "the least" of the earth.

In regard to the laity, the council stated that they, "by their very vocation, seek the kingdom of God by engaging in temporal affairs and by ordering them according to the plan of God."[18] This lifestyle may be accomplished in two ways; though in reality, they are interdependent. One way is for laypeople to look to their priest for direct guidance in decision-making and living. The second way is for them to take hold of the reins of responsible action and, "enlightened by Christian wisdom" and the "teaching authority of the Church," make their own paths in the world.[19]

The Medellín Conference

The Second General Conference of Latin American Bishops (CELAM) took place August 24-September 6, 1968, in Medellín, Colombia. Three years of implementing Vatican II had transpired. In those three years difficulties had arisen in the transformation of theory into practice. Political upheavals in various Latin American countries had occurred or were in the making. Intrigue and repression were rampant. Prevailing theories of developmentalism were being questioned. The need arose for the Church in Latin America to speak to these issues.

Paul VI convened the Medellín conference of Latin American bishops on August 24, 1968. This august occasion marked the first papal visit to Latin America. In his opening address, Paul VI briefly recounted the work that had been done in evangelization on their continent; but the work was not yet finished. A new strategy was necessary for evangelization to continue. The reason for this was obvious: "the labor already accomplished declares its own limitations, makes evident new necessities, demands something new and something great."[20]

Simply stated, the Church itself experiences:

the restlessness characteristic of our time, and particularly in those countries, straining towards their complete development, and troubled by the awareness of their economic, social, political and moral desequilibrium [sic].[21]

The Church can no longer ignore what is happening around it; but as the Body of Christ, the Church should not become directly involved in social and political issues. On the local level, however, its members are to be involved in the life of their country. In relation to this activity Paul promised to "promote the profound and far-sighted transformation of which . . . society has need."[22]

Inspired by such words, the bishops summarized their sixteen documents in seven commitments of the Latin American Church:

To inspire, encourage and press for a new order of justice that incorporates all men in the decision-making of their own communities;

To promote . . . the family, not only as a human sacramental community, but also as an intermediate structure in function of social change;

To make education dynamic in order to accelerate the training of mature men in their current responsibilities;

To encourage the professional organizations of workers, which are decisive elements in socio-economic transformation;

To promote a new evangelization and intensive catechesis that reach the elite and the masses in order to achieve a lucid and committed faith;

To renew and create new structures in the Church that institutionalize dialogue and channel collaboration between bishops, priests, religious and laity;

To cooperate with other Christian confessions, and with all men of good will who are committed to authentic peace rooted in justice and love.[23]

In the attempt to keep these commitments, "Latin America will undertake its liberation . . . in order to open itself to union with . . . the world . . . in a spirit of solidarity."[24]

This solidarity, especially in relation to the so-called developed nations, is based on the concept of "international justice," which is evidenced by the "recognition of the political, economic and cultural autonomy of our peoples."[25] In this way the internal activities of any given nation are the concern of that nation alone; that is to say, one nation may not impose its views of reality upon another. Assuming that all nations are attempting to institute a more just way of life for their people, every nation will engage in dialogue with the others.

On a superficial level it seems that the Latin American bishops have only reaffirmed much of what was said earlier at Vatican II.[26] But a closer reading of the Medellín documents reveals a different perspective for understanding and implementing Vatican II. According to Philip Berryman, a "Medellín methodology" was developed. It begins with an analysis of the socio-political reality in Latin America. Following this analysis comes a reflection upon that reality in light of the gospel. The process ends with appropriate pastoral recommendations. This methodology was used internally within the documents and externally in their ordering: from "Human Promotion" to "Evangelization and Growth in the Faith" to "The Visible Church and its Structures."[27]

The Method of Liberation Theology

To be completely honest, one cannot say that this "Medellín methodology" originated at the Medellín conference. The process of moving from an analysis of society to   reflection on the biblical text to efficacious action had been in use for several years throughout the Latin American continent.[28] The bishops gathered at Medellín only finalized its form; they provided sanction for a method already in use. To put it succinctly, for them "theology does not produce pastoral activity; rather, it reflects upon it."[29] A theology which follows upon the active participation of the minister in the life of the people will necessarily have characteristics that differ from one which precedes pastoral activity. The basic themes discussed here are not ranked in order of importance, for they emerged simultaneously from pastoral activity.

The Hermeneutic Circle

The first characteristic to be examined is the hermeneutic circle. Juan Luis Segundo defines it as "the continuing change in our interpretation of the Bible which is dictated by the continuing changes in our present-day reality, both individual and societal."[30] This hermeneutic is circular in that a new "present-day reality" causes a new interpretation of Scripture which results in a new reality, and so on. The expression "hermeneutic circle" should not be understood in a literal, two-dimensional way. It does not go around-and-around in the same rut; rather, like a spiral, it "keeps moving on towards an ever more authentic truth that is to be translated into ever more liberative praxis."[31]

These two poles of present-day reality and Scripture are connected by four steps. The first step is an ideological suspicion that results from a specific interpretation of God's Word which results in a changed experience of reality. Second, this suspicion is applied to the whole ideological superstructure, including theology. Third, this new theological experience leads to exegetical suspicion, that is, to the feeling that the prevailing interpretation of the Bible has left out some important pieces. Fourth, a new way of interpreting Scripture results, with new elements at the theologian's disposal.[32] According to J. Severino Croatto, these two poles cannot be separated in practice. He writes:

> the distinction between the two approaches is blurred and becomes simultaneous. What allows us to "enter" into the meaning of the text is the present event; from there on, even though we begin by approaching the biblical text, we are *already* "preunderstanding" it from the perspective of our existential situation.[33]

A corollary to the use of the hermeneutic circle is liberation theology's emphasis upon orthopraxis, the concrete behavior of Christians in the world. Gutiérrez points out that this re-emphasis upon orthopraxis is not to devalue or deny the need for orthodoxy; rather, it is to balance, and even to reject if necessary, the idolatry directed towards it.[34] Paraphrasing Marx, José Míguez Bonino argues that theology must stop defining the world and start transforming it. Liberation theologians believe that the situation in which Latin America exists today is partially the direct result of an orthodoxy that was not accompanied by orthopraxis. For them, "*orthopraxis*, rather than orthodoxy, becomes the criterion for theology."35

The Use of Marxism

Segundo argues that:

after Marx, our way of conceiving and posing the problems of society will never be the same again. . . . [Therefore], present-day social thought will be "Marxist" . . . that is, profoundly indebted to Marx.36

When one considers how far short the reality of capitalism has fallen in relation to its dream, it is no wonder that Bishop Antulio Parilla Bonilla can say: "Even a blind person can see that Latin America moves irreversibly toward some form of socialism."37

Míguez Bonino interprets this irreversible movement as a trend or "historical project" in Latin America. "Historical project" is an expression which refers to a middle ground between a utopia (a vision with no historical connection with the present) and a program (a developed model of social organization). An historical project is defined enough to force options in relation to society's structure, but is phrased in general, symbolic terms that cover many aspects and conceptions.38 Thus, while liberation theologians speak in terms of a "Latin American socialist project of liberation," they do not mean to imply an adoption of the political and economic structures of any existing socialist state. Their hope resides in the use of Marxist analysis and not in Marxism as it exists today. With Dom Helder Camara they say: "My socialism is a special one which respects the human person and turns to the gospel. My socialism is justice."39

The basic elements of this socialist historical project are sevenfold. First, it rejects "developmentalism" as an answer to Latin America's problems and attempts to break away from the North Atlantic states, that is, the United States and Europe, though not to the extent of isolationism. Second, this break is paralleled by a mobilization of "the people" to restructure Latin American society. Third, a strong centralized state is seen as a necessary step to counteract the inevitable hostile reactions from the North Atlantic states. Fourth, "the people" begin to take charge of their social structures, that is, they need to be "true protagonists of their own history." Fifth, since this will involve a prolonged struggle, the political dimension takes priority over all others.40 Sixth, though using Marxist categories and looking to existing socialist states, the goal is an authentic Latin American socialism. Seventh, this project is not merely economic or structural in nature; it intends to fashion a new humanity.41

The participation of Christians in this project is a fact.42 Their involvement is an attempt to live out their faith in love, a love that is not only compassion and comfort, but is also a love that seeks to change the world. So Míguez Bonino states:

in today's world there is only one way to feed the hungry, clothe the naked, care for the sick and imprisoned . . . [that is] to change the structures of society which create and multiply every day those conditions.[43]

Since these structures are the result of various forms of capitalism, the only possible answer seems to lie in socialism, which "represents the most fruitful and far-reaching approach."[44] Therefore, liberation theology is Marxist only in the sense that it appropriates Marxist categories. Marxism offers a way of analysis "open to the dynamism of history and to a projective view of human activity."[45]

Liberation theologians do not apply uncritically their Marxist critique to reality. It is utilized "totally and solely in the arena of human rationality--in the realm where God has invited man to be *on his own*."[46] Its target is the socio-economic and political reality of a specific point in time: Latin America today. Within this reality the political aspect is dominant, for politics is the means by which a society is constructed and "severely conditions all human activity."[47] Since this view of the use of Marxism corresponds to the Latin American situation, it becomes "*the unavoidable historical mediation* of Christian obedience."[48]

This radical statement leads to an equally radical conclusion: Christians, and therefore the church, must take sides in the quest for liberation. They either choose to act for liberation or choose against liberation by remaining neutral vis-à-vis the status quo. Unfortunately, the church usually does not recognize these two options. In the first place, the church does not want to identify itself with a Marxist ideology simply because it is "Marxist," and will thus break the unity of the church, which exists for all people. Second, there is the fear of calling the oppressed to work for their own liberation. Such an action would have two consequences: 1) it would cause the church to question its own privileged position in society; and 2) it might appear that the Body of the Prince of Peace would be sanctioning, and even participating in, a potentially violent class struggle.[49]

Despite the obvious self-protectiveness of the church's position, it reveals a correct understanding of the innate problems of political action. Choosing to move in one direction means not being able to move in another. It also reveals the depth of understanding the church has in regard to this central component of liberation theology; however, it also exposes a significant oversight on the part of the church: the goal of liberative political action is not merely social reorganization; it is also the formation of a new humanity. Thus, the church would do well to be more aware of what Gutiérrez refers to as the "three reciprocally interpenetrating levels of meaning" of the term liberation.

The first level relates to politics. Here, liberation reveals the:

aspirations of oppressed peoples and social classes, emphasizing the conflictual aspect of the economic, social and political process which puts them at odds with wealthy nations and oppressive classes.[50]

The second level refers to the understanding of history. By taking conscious responsibility for its destiny, humanity provides for itself:

a dynamic context and broadens the horizons of the desired social changes. .

. . [This] gradual conquest of true freedom leads to the creation of a new humankind and a qualitatively different society.51

The third, and deepest, level is Christ's liberation of humankind from sin, "which is the ultimate root of all disruption of friendship and of all injustice and oppression."52

Partisanship with
the Poor

This discussion of the possibility and viability of the church's taking a stand for liberation raises two important questions: 1) With which group is the church to identify? and 2) Does not taking sides with one group mean being against another? The second question is valid only if the ultimate goal of liberation is forgotten. If a new humanity is desired, then all persons must be moved to a new position; therefore, not only are the oppressed liberated from their obvious oppression, but oppressors are also liberated from their more subtle, though no less real, oppression. The answer to the first question is the subject of this section.

With whom is the church to stand? The final answer is the poor, the oppressed, the marginalized of society. They are the ones at the bottom of the pile. They are the ones who form the base of the hierarchical pyramid. They are the ones who have no foundation to stand upon. They are the ones who struggle to climb the ladder of success, to better themselves, all to no avail. They are the lower class.

Taking his lead from Calvin, Míguez Bonino declares:

Class struggle is a fact. . . . a war prompted by greed and power. . . . an effort of the dominating class to protect and maintain the present economic system beyond the time of its ability to provide for the basic needs of all mankind and to organize the productive forces of man and his technological discoveries in such a way that all men may realize their creative potentialities.53

Even though class struggle is a fact, it is not an essential part of nature; humanity will survive its eradication. Even in spite of its evil character, class struggle can play a positive role. It can be "a process through which the oppressed discover their identity and strength and consciously assume the struggle."54

The reality of class struggle raises an important question: "How is being human to be understood?" Or, put in another way: "What differentiates human being from other forms of being?" On the one hand, Marxism understands the human being fundamentally "as a worker, as the being who appropriates, transforms, and humanizes the world through his work and who himself comes to his own identity, becomes man through this same work."55 Stated this way, human being is rather one-dimensional and materially based. Traditional Christian anthropology, on the other hand, has understood human being in predominantly philosophical, cultural, and religious terms, thereby all but ignoring human work. Míguez Bonino contends there is a way of understanding human being that draws from the best of both positions. He argues that:

> whether one deals with the creation stories, with the law, or with the prophetic message, there seems to be in the Bible no relation of man to himself, to his neighbor, or even to God which is not mediated in terms of man's *work*.[56]

Even so, "work" must not be objectified into "works," understood in a theological sense. Objectification would take work out of its natural sphere and place it in a merit system, whereby value judgments would be made concerning the worker according to an evaluation of his or her work. This is what capitalism, in fact, does. It alienates people from their work. To be sure, this form of alienation is but a symptom of a deeper alienation, of a denial of one's humanity, that is, sin. But this assertion can only be made:

> in the context of a service . . . freely rendered, a work done "out of faith," outside the realm of worth and reward, in the anticipation of the realm of created love which is the Kingdom![57]

How does the church perform this service? How does the church stand with the poor? It does so through "an authentic imitation of Christ . . . which means taking on the sinful human condition to liberate humankind from sin and all its consequences."[58] This means, first of all, being in solidarity with the poor and protesting against poverty, that is, against the structures that cause deprivation of the basic necessities of life.[59] Secondly, it means that the church is:

> called to renounce self-defense and the struggle for power and to offer themselves, with the oppressed and on behalf of all, as signs of God's incoming new age of liberation and justice.[60]

The Base Communities

Liberation theology came to fruition within the *communidades eclesiales de base*, or base ecclesial communities. They are so named "because they are . . . primarily comprised of lower-class, grassroot people, the base of society" and the Church, that is, the laity.[61] According to Berryman, the base communities arose "out of a critical awareness of the inadequacy of existing pastoral models."[62] The fundamental problem was the increasing shortage of priests to minister to the people. Berryman cites two examples of "pastoral experimentation" as major antecedents for the base communities. The first one was "'specialized Catholic Action.'" In the 1950s, the Belgian priest Joseph Cardign developed a plan to reach young factory workers who were "outside the parish structure." Cardign formed small groups that were concerned with problems faced by the workers. The groups followed a methodology summarized by the words "'observe-judge-act.'" Observation occurred by the discussion of relevant fact. The group then decided whether or not the situation was consonant with the gospel. Finally, the group agreed to act in some way in response to their judgment.[63]

Berryman locates the second major antecedent in "church renewal movements," specifically the *Cursillos de Cristiandad* movement in Spain. *Cursillo* was (and is) an intense week-end retreat culminating in an "emotional conversion experience." Following this retreat, the *cursillistas* became involved in follow-up meetings and promoted the *cursillo* experience among their friends and associates. Many became "*cursillo* activists," that is, leaders of future *cursillo* conferences.[64]

The base communities are similar to these antecedents in three ways. First, they adopted the small group methodology which facilitated community and dialogue among the participants. Second, the base communities are primarily lay movements: priests and religious are advisors and resource persons. Third, they follow the observe-judge-act methodology, although on a wider scale.

The major difference between the base communities and their antecedents is the former's theological orientation. First, they were established in conscious imitation of the "house church" model found in the New Testament. Second, they function as the "focal point" for catechesis and evangelization. Third, base communities are almost exclusively composed of the rural poor, whereas their antecedents appealed to the middle and upper classes.[65] Yet, only a small proportion of the population participate in the base communities. Even where base communities thrive, as in Nicaragua and Brazil, only one or two percent of the people are involved.[66]

Building upon this foundation, Leonardo Boff posits five basic characteristics of the base communities. The first characteristic is "an oppressed yet believing people." The existence of base communities reflects the desire "to live more immediate and fraternal relationships."[67] They are composed of fifteen to twenty families which meet once or twice per week to study the Bible, share common problems, and solve them in light of Scripture. Each community structures its own worship and prayers, and decides what its tasks shall be. Thus, "the task of spreading the Gospel and keeping faith alive" becomes the responsibility of the laity.[68]

While recognizing the Church as Christ's gift to humanity, the base communities also embody the Church as the "human response to faith." Boff argues that "the Church is the People of God, born of a believing and, in many parts of the world, oppressed people through the Holy Spirit of God."[69] The institutional Church supports the base communities and, through them, enters into the "popular sector." In a similar way, the base communities remain a part of the institutional Church by their acceptance of the Church's clergy. Thus, there is no tension between the basic communities and the institutional Church. The real tension is between those in the Church who have opted for the poor and the ones who have not done so.[70]

Second, the base communities are "born from the Word of God." The gospel is their foundation. It is "heard, shared, and believed . . . and it is in its light that the participants reflect on the problems of their life."[71] The gospel is good news, "hope, promise, and joy" over against the actual life of the poor. The relationship between the gospel and life is a process. It begins with the problems faced by community members. Communal reflection on these problems evolves into an analysis of the community's immediate social milieu. This analysis leads the group to take a political stance vis-à-vis society. Finally, the community begins to participate in the struggle for liberation.[72]

"A new way of being Church" is Boff's third characteristic of the base communities. This should not be interpreted as a secession of the base communities from the institutional Church. Rather, it is a new way of being church within the structures of the Church.[73] Thus, Boff contends that, alongside its hierarchical structure:

> the Church is also an event. It emerges, is born, and is continually reshaped whenever individuals meet to hear the word of God, believe in it, and vow together to follow Jesus Christ, inspired by the Holy Spirit.[74]

This "new way" is evidenced by the radically democratic nature of the base communities. Everyone is an equal; "true brother and sister." But everyone does not do everything in the community. This gives rise to many different lay ministries or "services" within the group. In this way, "lay people are rediscovering their apostolic and missionary significance through the ecclesial communities."[75] It is the responsibility of the coordinator, often a woman, to provide order for the communities' life and worship.[76]

The base communities are also a "sign and instrument of liberation." They are not underground organizations. Group problems and solutions are discussed openly. Socio-political reality is recognized for what it is: "exploitation is exploitation; torture is torture; dictatorship is dictatorship."[77] This honesty is the basis for a new society "through the direct participation of all the members of the group, the sharing of responsibilities, leadership, and decision-making, through the exercise of power as service."[78] Therefore, the base communities are socially active. They are involved in solutions to local problems. On a larger scale they support "popular organizations" already in existence. Their activism often results in repression and persecution. But their suffering only serves to strengthen the faith and resolve of these communities.[79]

"A celebration of faith and life" is Boff's fifth characteristic of the base communities. The life of these groups is not exhausted by their prophetic denunciation of oppressive structures. They also take time to celebrate "the liberation that God achieved . . . in Jesus Christ; his presence through the word and the sacraments is celebrated and the faithful are comforted by his promises."[80] This is evidenced by the so-called "popular religiosity" of the people.[81] This phenomenon is the way "the people . . . nourish their trust while [living] in a society that has denied them their rights, dignity, and participation."[82] Thus, the celebrations of the base communities serve three purposes. First, they strengthen the faith of the people. Second, they "foster creativity" for the expression of their faith in life. Third, "liturgical creativity" is facilitated by the people's recognition of God's presence in the totality of life rather than being limited to the spiritual realm.[83]

Liberation: God's Work
    in History

        The final characteristic of liberation theology is also its goal, namely, God
has been working at liberation throughout history. This has been implicitly stated
in the preceding three sections. Segundo's point about the hermeneutic circle's
moving ever onward towards a more authentic truth points to this belief. If the
circle were truly circular, it would be only one social revolution following another.
Instead, it is social reorganization done in light of God's intention for humanity:
total liberation in which humanity is at one with itself and with God. Croatto
explicates this point from an exegetical point of view in his study of the Exodus and
its impact on the Judeo-Christian tradition.[84] Liberation from slavery, prophetic
denunciation of injustice and poverty, and the freedom that began with Christ--all
embody God's liberative intention within history.

        Theologians of liberation utilize Marxist categories because they provide a
way to analyze socio-political and economic systems that promote injustice and
impede liberation. Though they are critical of existing socialist states, these
theologians see the value of the theory behind their existence. Their hope is that
socialism will provide the means to implement the transformation of society and of
humanity that began with the embodiment of the kingdom in Jesus. Following his
example, liberation theologians critically assess the trends of the present age, noting
the places where they may minister to the needs that are present in appropriate
ways. Since it is difficult to hear the good news of the gospel amidst day-to-day
tragedy, their ministry begins with the prophetic denunciation of unjust systems.
Then, concrete examples of a new system are given which open the door for a more
traditional view of ministry.

Conclusion

        The roots and methodology of liberation theology impact its Christology in
several ways; some ways will be obvious while others are less clearly developed.
The task at hand is to give the reader guidelines, or a frame of reference, within
which to read the following chapters. The Second Vatican Council provides the
theological foundation for liberation Christology at several points. Latin Americans
reiterate the council's emphasis upon the holistic nature of the gospel; Jesus'
spiritual liberation has socio-political and economic implications. Liberation
Christology develops the council's "church of service" into its "church of the
poor," that is, a church focusing its ministry toward the oppressed and exerts its
influence on behalf of them.

        The Medellín Conference's influence is primarily methodological in that it
sanctioned the hermeneutic circle as a valid theological method. The three parts of
the circle--social analysis, theological reflection, and pastoral recommendations--are
reflected in Jesus' proclamation of God's kingdom and his call to discipleship. He
proclaims God's kingdom first to the poor and oppressed, thereby criticizing the
status quo. Thus, the conception of God behind Jesus' proclamation is God as a
God of life. Therefore, anyone who would follow Jesus is called to continue his

mission of proclaiming God's life-engendering rule first to the poor, and then to anyone else who will hear it.

If one depends upon explicit references to prove the influence of Marxist analysis on liberation Christology, one would conclude it has none. But it is there, in two critical concepts. The first is the result of an ideological suspicion vis-à-vis religious and political structures; namely, the depiction of the kingdom of God as the power for a radical transformation of the social order. This results in a new solidarity among the people and in a new humanity which embodies the kingdom values of love, justice, and mercy. This ideological suspicion also plays a major role in the interpretation of Jesus' death and its implication for his call to discipleship.

The base communities are the seedbed of liberation Christology. In these small groups, the people attempt to embody the liberation inherent in Jesus' proclamation of the kingdom of God. The base communities also provide the place for the realization of the three levels of liberation: 1) social analysis, including the redress of grievances, resulting in 2) the people becoming active subjects of their own history, all because 3) they have been liberated from sin and death by Jesus Christ.

The reader will also note the subjects of this chapter play an important part in the criticism of liberation Christology in chapter five. The influence of Marxism is denounced by Pope John Paul II, the Sacred Congregation for the Doctrine of the Faith, and Clark H. Pinnock. The Congregation also takes exception to the interpretation of Vatican II and to the role of the base communities in liberation Christology.

Notes

[1]For more detailed studies of this history see John A. Mackay, *The Other Spanish Christ: A Study of the Spiritual History of Spain and South America* (New York: Macmillan, 1932) and Enrique Dussell, *History of the Church in Latin America: Colonialism to Liberation*, trans. Donald D. Walsh (Grand Rapids: Eerdmans, 1981).

[2]On January 25, 1959, Pope John XXIII announced his intention to convoke the Twenty-First Ecumenical Council of the Roman Catholic Church. Vatican II began on October 11, 1962 and lasted until December 8, 1962. The second session, opened by Pope Paul VI, began on September 9, 1963 and closed December 4, 1963. September 14, 1964 and November 21, 1964 mark the beginning and ending dates of the third session. The final session began September 14, 1965 and concluded December 8, 1965. Whenever "Church" is used it refers to the Roman Catholic Church.

[3]Gender specific language will not be changed within quoted material.

[4]Vatican II, "Gaudium et Spes," n. 9, in Walter M. Abbott, gen. ed., *The Documents of Vatican II: All Sixteen Official Texts Promulgated by the Ecumenical Council 1963-1965* (New York: Herder and Herder, 1966). Cited hereafter as Vatican II.

[5]Vatican II, "Gaudium et Spes," n. 9.   [6]Ibid., n. 85.

[7]The various theories of development attempted to analyze Latin American economies and detail the ways they could become "developed" nations, that is, like the United States and Europe. For criticism of these theories, see Gustavo Gutiérrez, *A Theology of Liberation: History, Politics and Salvation*, rev. ed., trans. and ed. Sr. Caridad Inda and John Eagleson (Maryknoll: Orbis Books, 1988), pp. 13-25, cited hereafter as *Theology* and José Míguez Bonino, *Doing Theology in a Revolutionary Situation* (Philadelphia: Fortress Press, 1975), pp. 11-43, cited hereafter as *Doing Theology*. For examples of First World criticism, see Phillip Berryman, *Liberation Theology: Essential Facts about the Revolutionary Movement in Latin America and Beyond* (Oak Park, IL: Meyer Stone Books, 1987), pp. 3-8 and 111-124, cited hereafter as *Liberation Theology* and Jürgen Moltmann, "The Christian Theology of Hope and Its Bearing on Development" in *In Search of a Theology of Development: Papers from a Consultation on Theology and Development Held by SODEPAX in Cartigny, Switzerland, November, 1969* (Lausanne: Imprimerie La Concorde, ND), pp. 93-100.

[8]Vatican II, "Gaudium et Spes," n. 55.   [9]Ibid., n. 43.   [10]Ibid., n. 39.

[11]Ibid., n. 42.   [12]Ibid., n. 1.   [13]Vatican II, "Lumen Gentium," n. 8.

[14]Vatican II, "Gaudium et Spes," n. 22.   [15]Vatican II, "Lumen Gentium," n. 8.

[16]Ibid.   [17]Vatican II, "Presbyterorum Ordinis," n. 17.

[18]Vatican II, "Lumen Gentium," n. 31.   [19]Vatican II, "Gaudium et Spes," n. 43.

[20]Paul VI, "Opening Address to the Latin American Bishops' Conference" in CELAM, *The Church in the Present-Day Transformation of Latin America in the Light of the Council*, Vol. II (National Conference of Catholic Bishops: Washington, D.C., 1979), p. 3. Cited hereafter as CELAM.

[21]Ibid.   [22]Ibid., p. 15.

[23]CELAM, "Message to the People of Latin America," pp. 22-23.   [24]Ibid., p. 23.

[25]Ibid., p. 24.

[26]Some examples are the role of the laity, the bond of experience common to all people, the role of the Church as servant, and the importance of the political and economic realms of life.

[27]Phillip Berryman, *The Religious Roots of Rebellion: Christians in Central American Revolutions* (Maryknoll: Orbis Books, 1984), p. 27. Cited hereafter as *Religious Roots*.

[28]Cf. Ernesto Cardenal, *The Gospel According to Solentiname*, 4 vols., trans. and rev. Alan Neely (Maryknoll: Orbis Books, 1976-1982).

[29]Gutiérrez, *Theology*, p. 9.

[30]Juan Luis Segundo, *The Liberation of Theology*, trans. John Drury (Maryknoll: Orbis Books, 1976), p. 8. Cited hereafter as *Liberation*.

31Ibid. Therefore, the entry point of the hermeneutic circle is the reality which surrounds the theologian. For a Latin American theologian, it is the reality of oppression, repression, poverty, and dependence. Since these aspects of reality are a part of theologies, they become theological data alongside the Church's theological tradition. In actual practice social, political, and economic realities are the grids through which the Bible is read. Thus, the Bible becomes second in the hermeneutical process; but its interpretation is indispensable. Without it, present-day reality would remain the same: oppressive and inhuman.

32Ibid., p. 9.

33J. Severino Croatto, *Exodus: A Hermeneutic of Freedom*, trans. Salvator Attanasio (Maryknoll: Orbis Books, 1981), p. 82. Cited hereafter as *Exodus*.

34Gutiérrez, *Theology*, p. 8.   35Míguez Bonino, *Doing Theology*, p. 81.

36Luis Segundo, *Liberation*, p. 35, n. 10.

37Quoted in Míguez Bonino, *Doing Theology*, p. 38.   38Ibid., pp. 38-39.

39Quoted in ibid., p. 47.

40The emphasis upon politics is due to the fact that it is in this dimension that people live out their fundamental beliefs and have redress for their grievances.

41Míguez Bonino, *Doing Theology*, pp. 39-40.

42Cf. Berryman, *Religious Roots*, for an extensive exposition of this statement.

43Míguez Bonino, *Doing Theology*, p. 44.   44Gutiérrez, *Theology*, p. 55.

45Míguez Bonino, *Doing Theology*, pp. 34-35.   Thus, rigid Marxist orthodoxy or dogmatism is rejected. Marx and Lenin analyzed class structure as it appeared in northern European and Asian countries. But Latin America is subjected to multinational capitalism, which is different from nineteenth century capitalism. Therefore, Marxist categories need to be re-evaluated in light of this difference.

46Ibid., p. 98.   47Gutiérrez, *Theology*, p. 30.

48Míguez Bonino, *Doing Theology*, p. 99.   49Ibid., p. 57-58.

50Gutiérrez, *Theology*, p. 24.   51Ibid., pp. 24-25.   52Ibid., p. 25.

53Míguez Bonino, *Doing Theology*, p. 119.   54Ibid., p. 107.   55Ibid., p. 108.

56Ibid., p. 109.   57Ibid., p. 111.   58Gutiérrez, *Theology*, p. 172.

59Míguez Bonino, *Doing Theology*, p. 123.   60Ibid.

[61]Leonardo Boff, *Church: Charism and Power: Liberation Theology and the Institutional Church*, trans. John W. Diercksmeier (New York: Crossroad, 1985), p. 125. Cited hereafter as *Church*.

[62]Berryman, *Liberation Theology*, p. 68.   [63]Ibid., p. 65.   [64]Ibid., p. 66.

[65]Ibid., pp. 67-68.   [66]Ibid., p. 72.   [67]Boff, *Church*, p. 125.

[68]Ibid., pp. 125-26. Cf. Leonardo Boff, *Ecclesiogenesis: The Base Communities Reinvent the Church*, trans. Robert R. Barr (Maryknoll: Orbis Books, 1986), p. 4: "The [base] communities are built on a more vital, lively, intimate participation in a more or less homogeneous entity, as their members seek to live the essence of the Christian message: the universal parenthood of God, communion with all human beings, the following of Jesus Christ who died and rose again, the celebration of the resurrection and the Eucharist, and the upbuilding of the kingdom of God, already underway in history as the liberation of the whole human being and all human beings." Cited hereafter as *Ecclesiogenesis*.

[69]Boff, *Church*, p. 126.   [70]Ibid.   [71]Ibid., p. 71.   [72]Ibid.

[73]Cf. Boff, *Ecclesiogenesis*, p. 7: "*The church sprung from the people is the same as the church sprung from the apostles.*"

[74]Boff, *Church*, p. 127.   [75]Ibid., p. 128.

[76]Ibid., pp. 127-28. Cf. Boff, *Ecclesiogenesis*, p. 5, where Boff acknowledges the fact that, in every community, "there is always a power structure, in either the dominative or the solidarity version. . . . Realistically, one can only struggle for a type of sociability in which love will be less difficult, and where power and participation will have better distribution."

[77]Boff, *Church*, p. 128.   [78]Ibid.   [79]Ibid., pp. 128-29.   [80]Ibid., p. 129.

[81]Boff defines popular religiosity as "the devotions to the particular saints of the people, the processions, and other popular feasts" (ibid.). See also Berryman, *Liberation Theology*, pp. 69-71.

[82]Boff, *Church*, p. 130. On the importance of celebration, see also Jürgen Moltmann, "The Liberating Feast," trans. Francis McDonagh in *Politics and Liturgy*, eds. Herman Schmidt and David Power (New York: Herder and Herder, 1974), pp. 74-84.

[83]Boff, *Church*, p. 130. Boff examined the base communities in depth in his book, *Ecclesiogenesis*. Specifically, he discussed "the ecclesiality of these communities, their contribution to a transcendence of the church's current structure and, as *quaestiones disputatae*, the historical Jesus and the institutional forms of the church, the possibility of a lay person celebrating the Lord's Supper, and women's priesthood and its possibilities" (p. 3).

[84]Severino Croatto, *Exodus*.

Chapter 2

JESUS CHRIST, THE CHRISTIC CENTER OF REALITY:
THE CHRISTOLOGY OF LEONARDO BOFF

This chapter is concerned with the Christology of Leonardo Boff. It begins with a biographical sketch of his life, followed by a critical analysis of his Christology. The chapter ends with a discussion of the impact of his Christology on his theology.

Biographical Sketch

Leonardo Boff was born on December 14, 1938, in Concordia, Brazil. He studied philosophy and theology in both Curitiba and Petrópolis. On December 15, 1964, he was ordained a Franciscan priest. He specialized in systematic theology at the universities of Oxford, Wurzburg, Louvain, and Munich. He received a doctorate in theology from Munich in 1972. His dissertation was entitled *Die Kirche als Sakrament im Horizont der Welterfahrung*. Boff is presently professor of systematic theology at the Petropolis Institute of Philosophy and Theology. He is an editor of *Revista Eclesiastica Brasileira*, the Portuguese edition of *Concilium*, and the coordinator for theological publications of the Franciscans' Editôra Vozes. Boff is also a theological assessor for the Latin American Conference of Religious, the Brazilian Conference of Religious, the Brazilian Conference of Bishops, and the National Pastoral Institute, an organization connected with the Brazilian Conference of Bishops.

Boff has published more than thirty books and articles in the last fifteen years. He is also a proponent of liberation theology. On May 15, 1984, Boff was called to Rome by Joseph Cardinal Ratzinger, prefect of the Sacred Congregation for the Doctrine of the Faith, concerning his book, *Church: Charism and Power*. On May 2, 1985, Boff received the official result of his conversation with Ratzinger: 1) a one year's "silence under obedience"; 2) a renunciation of his editorial duties on *Revista Eclesiastica Brasileira*; and 3) a censorship on any theological writing during his "silence." Exempt from the ban were homilies at the Eucharist and theological lectures to Franciscan seminarians in Petrópolis, as the latter were closed to the public. Boff's "silence" ended March 29, 1986.[1]

Jesus Cristo Libertador was written in 1972, a time of political oppression in Brazil. The word "liberation" could not be used because of its revolutionary overtones. In the English translation, Boff added an epilogue in order to "underline the liberative dimensions present in the life, message, and practical activity of the historical Jesus."[2] The book has several purposes: 1) to condense and systematize several years of christological reflection; 2) to present a Christology that was relevant to its Brazilian and Latin American *Sitz im Leben*; and 3) to:

help more privileged Christians join in fellowship with those who are more oppressed, to commit themselves to the messianic task of liberating human beings completely from everything that diminishes them and offends God.[3]

Methodology

Even though liberation theology is explicitly situation-oriented, it did not emerge from a theological vacuum. The history of theology has played an important role in its formation. In relation to Christology, each generation has attempted to answer Jesus' question, "Who do people say I am?" within the context of its understanding of the results of the history of Christology. No single answer to, or interpretation of, Jesus is satisfactory for today. But Boff does not wish to overlook anything positive that history has to offer.[4]

The History of
  Christology

Boff critically examines nine theological movements, six of which he implicitly engages in dialogue throughout his Christology. The first answer to Jesus' question is that of "imperturbable faith," that is, traditional Christology: Jesus of Nazareth is the Christ, the only begotten and eternal Son of God, sent to liberate humanity from its sins; he died a sorrowful death; arose from the dead, thereby substantiating his claim as Son of Man, Son of God, and the Messiah. To a certain extent, this is Boff's final conclusion. But the means by which he arrives there, and the meaning he attaches to those means, separates him from this traditional stance.

The second answer began with the Enlightenment and continues today. Basically, it concerns the historical Jesus-Christ of faith dichotomy. The Gospels were seen as theological interpretations of Jesus rather than historical biographies. Some rejected the historicity of Jesus and posited Christ as a projection of the human longing for liberation. Others suggested a difference between Jesus and Christ, and began to look for a Jesus not yet interpreted as Christ or tied to cult and dogma.

Rudolf Bultmann deduced from this that theology should focus solely upon the Christ of faith. The only relevant facts about Jesus for faith are that he lived and that he was crucified. The so-called post-Bultmannians, however, marked a return to the historical Jesus, albeit a critical one. They were concerned with the connection between the historical Jesus and the Christ of faith. According to Boff, their research branched into 1) Jesusology, how Jesus understood himself and allowed others to understand him through words and acts, and 2) Christology, the clarification of the later community's belief about Jesus.[5]

A movement popular among Roman Catholic theologians is a philosophical-transcendental one. This view sees in Jesus' humanity an openness to, and longing for, God that is present in all people. Jesus of Nazareth is not the only realization of this human longing for God. He is, however, its definitive concretion. Boff draws a major motif of his Christology from this interpretation: Jesus is the epitome of what constitutes human being. In his exalted state, Jesus Christ is at work throughout the cosmos, personal and impersonal, facilitating the union between God and creation.[6]

The cosmic-evolutionist interpretation of Jesus popularized by Teilhard de Chardin and his followers is also important to Boff. As the Omega point, Jesus Christ is both the greatest gift creation can give to God and the greatest gift God gives to humanity. Boff uses this view to deepen the relationship between God and humanity throughout history.[7]

The final interpretation of Jesus that significantly impacts Boff's Christology is a secular, socio-critical interpretation. This view uncovered how individualistic and separated from the social and political world Jesus' message had become in traditional Christologies. Jesus' life, actions, and language had social and political implications. Boff continually refers to the fact that the kingdom which Jesus announced calls for a complete transfiguration of individuals, societies, and the cosmos.[8]

The Hermeneutic Problem

The history of Christology raises the question of the way Jesus Christ may be known. For Boff, this means one must confront the Gospels. This confrontation raises the issue of hermeneutics, which is more than the art of understanding ancient texts. It includes also an understanding of life and knowing how to relate it to these texts. This understanding occurs on both the individual and the collective levels, where themes such as the kingdom of God, justice, peace, and reconciliation express the hopes of human nature.[9]

Boff analyzes several types of hermeneutics in order to glean from them a hermeneutic appropriate to Latin America. One type that Boff uses to interpret the Gospels' presentation of Jesus is historical criticism. Since this methodology is well known, there is no need to discuss it here. Suffice it to say that Boff is unafraid to apply these tools to the New Testament witness to Jesus.

Boff does not use this method uncritically. Its basic limitation is its claim to neutrality resulting in an objectifying of the subject. Comprehension, on the other hand, implies knowledge from personal involvement and commitment to the subject. Comprehension always involves interpretation. Thus, one approaches an object with a precomprehension derived from one's cultural milieu, education, and traditions. Precomprehension does not equal preconception. The former takes into account one's conditioning factors, and remains open to questioning from the object. The latter unconsciously takes its conditioning factors into the encounter, but is not open to judgment.[10]

This has several ramifications for Christology. First, one approaches Jesus from the standpoint of faith, from personal involvement and commitment to Jesus. Second, Jesus is known through the community of faith. Boff contends that:

> it is within the church that an atmosphere of faith was created, that the Gospels were written, and that the common coordinates by which we confront and situate ourselves before Christ were established.[11]

Finally, Jesus has entered the substratum of western culture. Here, in the collective unconscious, the cosmic Christ is at work prolonging the Incarnation of Jesus that began in Nazareth and continues until it is fulfilled in the kingdom of God.[12]

This understanding of incarnation led to another type of hermeneutics: one of "political existence." This hermeneutic recognizes that ideologies (understood in a pejorative way) may enter the church or culture influenced by Christ. The results are disastrous: maintaining the status quo, shutting off the possibility of growth, prohibiting self-criticism, and disallowing the gospel to be a "disturbing ferment" among the people.[13] In other words, the presence of ideologies goes against the fact that Christ came:

> to create an atmosphere, a love and reciprocity that ought to be realized in all situations, in all social and political systems and in every articulation of religion or morality.[14]

Boff also draws upon what he calls "the hermeneutic of salvation history." Salvation history "is understood as a history of self-communication on the part of God and as a history of the human responses to the divine proposal."[15] Creation is the pre-condition for God's self-communication and, in fact, ought to be understood initially as a part of God's self-communication. A dialectic exists between God's proposal and human response. The former can never be achieved fully within history. It can only be grasped through historical models which represent "specific mediation[s]" between God's proposal and human response. Even though verbal forms, language, and meanings of words change, care should be taken to insure that the intent of the original work is maintained in the translation process.[16]

Toward a Latin American Christology

One point must be made clear before channeling these hermeneutical approaches into one stream. Boff contends that Jesus cannot be spoken about as if he were the object in a subject-object dichotomy. Christians "can only speak *with him as starting point*, as people touched by the significance of his reality."[17] Not merely as "people" understood in a generic way, but as people who have been touched within their own socio-historical context. Therefore, Boff's interpretation of Christ will be a Latin American one. Such a Christology will have five general characteristics. It should be noted that these characteristics entail a re-ordering of priorities without excluding some in favor of a total preoccupation of others.

The first characteristic is "the primacy of the anthropological element over the ecclesiastical." The Church in Latin America structured itself according to

European standards. The faith it expounded was artificial for Latin America, that is, it:

> basically impeded healthy attempts to create a new incarnation of the church outside of the inherited traditional framework of a Greco-Roman understanding of the world.[18]

To counterbalance this tendency, a Latin American Christology needs to focus on the human person that the church is meant to serve.[19]

"The primacy of the utopian element over the factual" is the second characteristic of a Latin American Christology. Boff contends that "the determining element in the Latin American person is not the past ([that is,] colonization) but the future."[20] Utopia is not an illusion, but is born of hope. Utopia engenders models permanently open to transformation, not absolutization. These models serve as means of anticipation of the definitive world promised and demonstrated by Jesus Christ.[21]

Another characteristic is "the primacy of the critical element over the dogmatic." A Latin American Christology should recognize that "the general tendency of people, and in particular of institutions, is to stagnate in an existential arrangement that was successful during a specific period."[22] The narrowing of horizons is the inevitable result of stagnation. This element helps to keep incarnate the core of Christian experience within history.[23]

The fourth characteristic is "the primacy of the social over the personal" element. The greatest problem Latin America faces is the marginalization of the majority of its population. This problem cannot be solved solely by personal conversion, for structural evil transcends personal evil. The church must decide where it will stand. According to Boff, the church:

> should emphasize the future that [Christ] promises for this world, a world in which the future kingdom is growing between the wheat and the cockle, not for a few privileged people, but for all.[24]

"Primacy of orthopraxis over orthodoxy" is the final characteristic of a Latin American Christology. Boff contends that the greatest weakness of classical Christology is its theological-philosophical systematization. What one thought about Christ was more important than acting in light of him. Thus, even though the church preached Christ, the Liberator, it was often ambivalent towards liberation movements. This ambivalence caused an exodus of the "best" people from the church. Boff believes this element can help to reverse this trend by providing a Christian outlet for political activism.[25]

There are two ways these characteristics, in conjunction with Scripture and tradition, may be developed into a Latin American Christology. Boff calls one way a "sacramental articulation of liberation Christology." He calls it sacramental "because in the facts of real life it symbolically intuits the presence of oppression and the urgent need for liberation."[26] Poverty is a social evil God does not will; Christian obedience demands its annihilation. Prophetic denunciation and hortatory proclamation characterize the language of this Christology. A praxis of committed love is its necessary lifestyle. More power needs to be given to the dominated people. A Christology of this sort:

> examines and gives special emphasis to all the gestures, words, and attitudes of Jesus that have to do with conversion, a change in existing relationships, a rapprochement with those on the outer margins of Jewish society, a predilection for the poor, a willingness to challenge the religious and social status quo of his day, and the political content of his proclamation of God's kingdom. The factors that led to his death also take on special relevance. The result is an image of Christ the Liberator quite different from that of official dogma, that of popular piety centered around the suffering and downtrodden Christ of the passion, and also the image of Christ as the glorious king in heaven.[27]

The second type of Christology possible is a "socio-analytical articulation of liberation Christology." This approach begins with the same social, political, economic, and religious context as the first. Its difference resides in the fact that "it attempts to detect the mechanisms that generate such scandalous poverty and to elaborate a praxis that is liberative and effective."[28] Thus, the theory behind this Christology has two parts. The first is social analysis, which examines the reality to be changed. The second is hermeneutics, which relates this social analysis to the word of divine revelation in Jesus Christ.

This is the type of liberation Christology that Boff seeks to elaborate. The reading of his christological works makes it clear that he is mainly concerned with the hermeneutical aspect of Christology. It is just as obvious that he has been influenced by the social analysis that has preceded his work.[29] The planting of seeds and the cultivation of tender, young shoots is past. The time of harvest is at hand.

Jesus of Nazareth

Since Jesus is the starting point for liberation Christology, Boff finds it necessary to ask a very pointed question right at the beginning: "What did Jesus Christ really want to bring, and what did he actually bring to us?" Boff frames his answer in the broadest terms possible: "Jesus Christ wants to be in his own person God's answer to the human condition."[30] Both the question and its answer sound very traditional, which they are to a certain degree. But this "human condition" is not to be understood in a universal way. Rather, it is the condition of being human in Latin America today. To be sure, Latin Americans, like North Americans and Europeans, want happiness in life, to love and to be loved, and desire peace; but their history, their cultures, and sub-cultures give a unique slant to this question and its answer.

The Kingdom of God
as Utopia

Boff begins his explication of this situation with an analysis of Jesus' proclamation of the kingdom of God. The phrase "kingdom of God" "signified that God is the ultimate meaning of this world; God will intervene shortly and restore the foundations of all creation, establishing a new heaven and a new earth."[31] Thus, the kingdom of God was a sign of hope for Jesus' listeners. It signified a hope that at the end of the world all alienation and evil would be overcome; that hate, divisions, death, that is, the consequences of sin, would be destroyed. In other words, God's sovereignty over satanic forces would be manifested.

For Boff, God's kingdom is "utopia." Utopia originally meant "no place"; but in Jesus, God was making the kingdom "topia," a specific place. That "topia" is where freedom and liberty are proclaimed, sight is given to the blind, the lame walk, and good news is preached to the poor (Lk. 4:18-19; Mt. 11:5). Historically speaking, this utopia of the jubilee was never fulfilled. It gradually came to be seen as a promise to be fulfilled by the Messiah; therefore, whoever does such signs is the Liberator of humanity. For Boff, "Christ understands himself as Liberator because he preaches, presides over, and is already inaugurating the kingdom of God."[32] Boff contends that God's kingdom is not the creation of a new world; rather, it is the transformation of the existing one. The kingdom is not merely the annihilation of sin; it is also the annihilation of all that sin means: pain, death, blindness, and hunger.[33]

Two conclusions may be drawn from this. First, the kingdom of God is a new order, a new way of being, rather than a territory. When Jesus says, "The kingdom is among you," he means the new order is here now. To ask about its future establishment is to act as if it were a place. Openness to God's leadership corrects this misunderstanding; therefore, the kingdom is dynamic. It reveals God's intervention here and now, though it is not yet fully realized. The future aspect of the kingdom remains to be seen, for its fulfillment depends upon God, not humanity.[34]

The second conclusion follows from the first: God's kingdom is not merely spiritual. Jesus' proclamation of the kingdom meant that "the totality of this material world, spiritual and human . . . is now introduced into God's order."[35] If this were not true, if the kingdom were not holistic, then the following that Jesus gained is inexplicable; but multitudes did follow him. They believed the eschaton had begun in him, that he belonged to God's kingdom, and that their following him guaranteed their participation in the new order.[36]

This raises the issue of apocalypticism, which cannot be ignored when dealing with Jesus' proclamation of the kingdom. Why did Jesus choose apocalyptic language as a vehicle for his message? Part of the answer lies in the fact that Jesus was a man of his time. The other part relates to the people. According to Josephus' *Antiquities*, the Jewish people from 100 B.C.E. to 100 C.E. were preoccupied by the thought of being "liberated from all kinds of domination by others, so that God alone might be served."[37] The political reality of those two centuries did little to foster the hope of self-governance. Only a direct intervention by God could realize it. Apocalyptic literature arose "to inspire confidence in the people and open up the possibility of a way out."38

"Kingdom of God," read theocratically as "Reign of God," abounded in the literature of the time. The political connotations were obvious: "God's lordship over all had also to be demonstrated politically."39 The people prepared themselves for God's reign in many ways: the Pharisees by their strict adherence to the Law; the Essenes and Qumranites by separation and purification; the Zealots by guerrilla warfare. In order to be God's answer to the human condition Jesus used messianic and apocalyptic language to communicate his liberating message to the people of his day.

In spite of the well-known discontinuities between Jesus and apocalypticism, Boff contends that Jesus' wilderness temptation to political messianism was a real one for him. Had he succumbed to this temptation, the kingdom would have been "particularized and reduced to a part of reality, such as politics."40 Its universality would have been lost. This temptation had ramifications for Jesus' entire life. Boff puts the matter this way:

> The great drama of the life of Christ was to try to take the ideological content out of the word "kingdom of God" and make the people and his disciples comprehend that he signified something much more profound, namely, that he demands a conversion of persons and a radical transformation of the human world; that he demands a love of friends and enemies alike and the overcoming of all elements inimical to God and humankind.41

In other words, Jesus made the kingdom of God a reality, not merely a utopia.

Kingdom Demands

Again, in relation to the kingdom, Jesus makes two demands: personal conversion and restructuring of the human world. Conversion, a change in one's "thinking and acting to suit God," implies a rupture in one's life. But this rupture is to be life-giving, leading one to a crisis and to deciding for a new order, which is Jesus himself. A decision for Jesus means becoming as a child, totally dependent upon God in light of the kingdom's demands. It means developing an "attitude of readiness to comply with the exigencies of Jesus."42 This attitude places one in a tenuous position vis-à-vis the Law, for freedom results in service for good rather than in libertinism. As Boff says, "Christ is not *against* anything. He is in favor of love, spontaneity, and liberty."43

Obviously, living in the freedom that Jesus gives is much more difficult than living in legalism. It takes a tremendous amount of "creative imagination" for one to decide how to give oneself in service to others. The result is a radical formula: the Sermon on the Mount. Boff criticizes interpretations that see this formula as an interim ethic or as sayings that affect people's attitudes but not their actions. For him, the Sermon on the Mount is not a law. Laws seek to promote harmony among people. They do so with the threat of retributive justice. But Jesus' teaching breaks this circle. Instead of retributive justice, he says that all are worthy of love. At bottom, the Sermon on the Mount is a "catechism of comportment" for the disciple who is seeking to construct norms that conform to the divine lifestyle Jesus brought.[44]

Jesus' preaching of the kingdom of God demands a conversion of individuals which, in turn, affects the world around them. This social change is accomplished "in terms of a liberation from legalism, from conventions without foundations, from authoritarianism and the forces and powers that subject people."[45] This was reflected in Jesus' relationship with the scribes and Pharisees. They were not evil people. They did what the Law and society required to be called good. What they did not realize was that participation in the status quo did not guarantee entry into the kingdom. A change is required. Jesus followed the spirit of the Law (love, justice, and mercy) to effect this change in people and society. He began with outcasts and sinners, who readily listened to him because they were nothing, that is, they had nothing to lose and everything to gain. So, in spite of "official" opposition, Jesus continued to preach individual and social conversion because the ultimate end, the kingdom, "is close at hand."[46]

The relationship that is established among people who respond positively to Jesus' message is obvious: they are brothers and sisters to one another and citizens of God's kingdom. But Boff takes this a step further. To him, "there are no more friends or enemies, neighbors or strangers. There are only brothers and sisters."[47] One reason for this universalization is due to the work of the cosmic Christ.[48] Another is that the followers of Jesus:

> inaugurate a new type of human being and humanism, one we believe to be the most perfect that has ever emerged; and it has the capacity to assimilate new and different values without betraying its own essence.[49]

It is possible to understand Boff's position in a syncretistic, universalist manner; but that would be missing the point. Not every aspect of religious belief and practice, not even of Christianity, is appropriate kingdom behavior. Only those beliefs and practices that foster love and facilitate its growth, humanize the human condition, and liberate people to be fully human are the ones that can be assimilated without betraying Jesus. Boff puts it this way: "In the important questions of life nothing can substitute for the human person: neither law, nor traditions, nor religion."[50]

Jesus: the Epitome of
the Human Being

Boff takes very seriously the Chalcedonian affirmation that Jesus is "truly man." Whether or not sinfulness is innately human is not an issue here.[51] Suffice it to say at this point that Jesus "already presents himself as a new man, as of a new creation reconciled with itself and with God."[52] Within this newness Boff sees three human characteristics elevated to new heights: "good sense, creative imagination, and originality." His explication of these points is grounded entirely on the preceding discussion of conversion from legalism to the "law" of love.

For Boff, good sense is being able to see to the core of things and knowing the way to verbalize it. This ability arises from a concrete knowledge, or experience, of life. Such knowledge means that "God, human beings, society, and nature are immediately present to [Jesus]."[53] He does not theologize, moralize, or get bogged down in heartless casuistry; but his words encounter the world in such a way as to force a decision before God. The call to decision does not come from on high, or only to a select few. It may be experienced in everyday things: a city set on a hill cannot be hid; each day has its own troubles. Good sense and sound reason, available to all, reveal these things.

Nor did Jesus appeal to a higher, outside authority. His words carried their own weight. Yet, he did not say new things to make a name for himself. Instead, "he brings to light that which people always knew or ought to have known but because of their alienation were unable to see, comprehend, and formulate."[54] Jesus used ordinary, everyday things to expound the will of God because he was seeking understanding from his hearers.[55]

Boff asserts that Jesus possessed a creative imagination. This should not be understood as dreams, passing illusion, or flight from reality--quite the contrary. Creative imagination:

> is born in confrontation with reality and established order; it emerges from nonconformity in the face of completed and established situations; it is the capacity to see human beings as greater and richer than the cultural and concrete environment that surrounds them; it is having the courage to think and say something new and to take hitherto untreaded paths that are full of meaning for human beings.[56]

Thus, Jesus walks and talks with sinners, and even surrounds himself with such people. He turns the social and religious framework upside down: the last shall be first; the humble shall be rulers. While salvation is offered to all, it is sinners who joyfully respond to its offer.[57]

In Jesus' "imaginative" proclamation of God's kingdom, Boff maintains that he never used the word "obedience," for the word connotes adherence to a law.[58] At worst, it means legalism. For obedience to be applied to the kingdom demands made by Jesus it cannot be "a question of fulfilling orders, but a firm decision in favor of what God demands within a concrete situation."[59] Preconception and prejudice have no place here. Love is the only way to relate to people. Drawing on the judgment scene in Matthew 25, Boff writes: "The sacrament of brotherhood is absolutely necessary for salvation. Those who deny this deny the cause of Christ."[60]

At bottom, Jesus is an original. This does not imply that he always said and did completely new things; rather, his originality stems from his relation to the Origin. Jesus is an original because through his life, words, and deeds he brought "others to the origin and root of their own selves" by speaking "of things with absolute immediacy and superiority."[61] In other words, Jesus placed people in a crisis of decision: be converted to God's work or be a part of the secondary, current situation.[62]

A positive response to the person of Jesus is a bittersweet one. On the one hand, it is a liberation from the bondage of things that were meant to serve rather than be served. It opens up new possibilities for relating to oneself, God, others, and creation. On the other hand, living for others means turning away from structures and institutions that give the impression of necessity and divine sanction. For Boff, to be a disciple of Jesus "means liberation and the experience of a new redeemed and reconciled life. But it can also include, as in the case of Christ, persecution and death."[63]

Before discussing the death of Jesus, Boff's view of the relationship between Christology and soteriology requires examination. The former is concerned with the person of Jesus and the latter with his saving work. Boff does not deal with this relationship directly. One may surmise from his methodology that Christology has precedence. Even when discussing salvation Boff grounds it upon his vision of who Jesus is. Thus, Boff agrees with Wolfhart Pannenberg, that "soteriology must follow from Christology."[64]

Even while saying this Pannenberg issues a warning: culture determines one's reading of Scripture and, therefore, of the life of Jesus. In other words, what one desires most is what one finds in Scripture. Boff is not excluded from this danger. His culture feels the need for liberation from oppression, for an affirmation of its humanity, along with the traditional understanding of salvation. He finds this in Jesus the Liberator. If this is eisegesis, then every generation and every culture is guilty of it, for every interpretation of salvation is culture-specific. To this writer, Boff is not engaging in eisegesis. What he has done is find a new way to express for Latin Americans "the fact that in Jesus the destiny of man in general has found its fulfillment."[65]

Jesus' Death: The Crime and its Meaning

Boff's discussion of the death of Jesus is both familiar and foreign. Its familiarity is evident at several points: his source is Scripture, most notably the Gospel of Mark; he utilizes the findings of New Testament exegetes and theologians; he engages in a lively discussion with systematic theologians on the meaning of the passion. On the other hand, Boff's discussion is never more liberation-oriented than here: Jesus' death is the direct result of his nonconformity vis-à-vis the religious and political establishments of his day; Boff's language is that of modern terrorism and totalitarian regimes: interrogation, torture, execution, and guerrilla fighter characterize his description of the passion. One quickly perceives that Jesus' death and ensuing resurrection are pivotal points for Boff's Christology. The crucifixion reveals the depth and power of structural sin, and the complex networking it will undertake to preserve its privileged position. The resurrection reveals God's final, albeit proleptic, judgment of corporate sin and, by implication, of the status quo.

Boff is not a disinterested expositor of the passion. The death of Jesus is an event that strikes at the heart of one who claims to be a Christian in Latin America today. As a Latin American, Boff contends that three contextual experiences govern his understanding of the crucifixion:

> 1. The experience of *political, economic, and cultural oppression* of one group by another group. . . . [which] consists of hunger, misery, institutionalized international crime, enormously destructive wars, a division between wealthy countries and poor countries--in a word, it amounts to a situation of world injustice.

> 2. The experience of *liberation movements,* which seek to shake off all yokes and go in search of a new manner of life in common, seek to gestate a new type of human being, one who will be more of a comrade, more open to communion.

> 3. The experience of *resistance* on the part of dominated but undefeated groups working in a regime of captivity and refusing to let the spark of hope flicker and die.[66]

Alongside these contextual interests Boff places four interests evident within the Gospel accounts themselves.

> 1. The texts as we have them were written considerably after the paschal event, and in light of the major fact of the resurrection. . . . In light of the resurrection, the primitive community entered upon the process of interpreting the whole life of Christ.

> 2. Side by side with this general perspective, that of the resurrection, there is also an apologetic, internal moment. First the phenomenon of Jesus Christ must be rendered intelligible to Jewish converts.

> 3. The literary genre of the passion narratives is precisely that of *account.* The passion is being *told, recounted* . . . not in terms of the criteria of modern historiography--but nonetheless with the guiding interest of recounting. . . . the suffering and passion of Jesus, who was the messiah.

> 4. The *Sitz im Leben* . . . of the accounts is liturgical. . . . Christians in their gatherings recalled and meditated on the great moments of the Lord's life, death, and resurrection.[67]

From these two sets of interests Boff discusses the passion and draws from it its meaning for Latin America today. This meaning is overtly political, for Boff contends that the historical causes and political dimensions of Jesus' death play a primary role in the passion.

As stated above, Boff holds that Jesus' death is the direct result of his praxis; but the content of his praxis must be understood in the context in which Jesus found himself. After the Babylonian exile, the Jews had only one brief respite from political oppression. Rome's presence was felt everywhere in the forms of its occupation army and a network of tax collectors; which also helped shape another oppression, a socio-economic one. The Roman tax system was onerous, complex, and universal. Jewish tradition also contributed to the problem.

The double patrimony of Mosaic law provided a surplus of workers which resulted in a lower quality of life for most of the population. In fact, adherence to the Law resulted in an oppression of a religious nature. Instead of facilitating the meeting of the people with God, it had degenerated into a barrier between the two.

It was into this world, with its three-dimensional oppression, that Jesus came preaching the kingdom of God, "an ultimate end, one that calls into question social, political, and religious interests."[68] His new praxis started a six-step process of "partial liberations" designed to deliver human beings from their oppressed life. The first step in this process was the "relativization of human self-sufficiency," self-sufficiency understood as the gaining of salvation by following the law and its traditions. At this point Jesus stands firmly in the prophetic tradition that said love, justice, and mercy are more important than sacrifice. Religion, then, is not a substitute for one's neighbor; rather, it should inculcate "a permanent orientation to genuine love of the other--in whom, incognito, God is hidden."[69]

The second step is the "creation of a new solidarity," which is the direct result of this "deabsolution" of religion. Jesus toppled the class structure of his day by associating with sinners and entering into solidarity with the oppressed; nor is he concerned with the consequences of this action. It is by this type of love "that one learns the meaning of the reign of God, and of liberation from the structures of oppression that discriminate between human being and human being."[70]

The next phase follows from the second: a new "respect for the freedom of others." Jesus gave people a chance to speak, to question, to define themselves. In return, Jesus works with people and teaches by example. He does not resort to the power of authority but speaks persuasively to conscience.[71]

Activities such as these inevitably evoke conflict. The fourth step is Jesus' "inexhaustible capacity to bear up under conflict." He continually aided those who were "sinners" in the eyes of the social and religious establishments. Even so, he travelled among the oppressors, extending the possibility of salvation to them, also. All persons, friend or enemy, are to be treated with respect while the enslaving structure is to be given no quarter.[72]

The fifth step in the process of Jesus' liberative praxis is the "acceptance of mortality." Jesus accepted life as it came to him and lived it as a being-for-others. Death is not merely the cessation of biological life; it is also the ultimate opportunity for one to accept freely the finitude of life by opening oneself up to something greater than death and someone greater than life. Thus, Jesus' entire life was an acceptance of death.[73]

The final step is actually a process within a process, for it extends through the entire span of Jesus' life. It is his experience of God as "Abba." For Jesus, God was "a Father of infinite goodness and limitless love for all human beings, especially for the ungrateful and the wicked, the wandering and the lost."[74] This included everyone, both those whom society and religion labeled "sinners" and those who, in reality, were sinners. Jesus embodied this love by bringing the goodnews of God's kingdom to all persons: rich and poor, male and female, oppressed and oppressor, friend and foe.

As far as the passion events themselves are concerned, Boff reveals his involvement with, and indebtedness to, modern New Testament exegesis. He does not shrink from pointing out sayings or events that reflect the theology of the early church rather than historical events. Jesus' predictions of his death are examples of this. Boff also follows many exegetes by holding that Mark's account is the oldest and most historically accurate; but this does not blind him to the fact that this is a theological account of the last days of Jesus' life. For example, a post-resurrection faith could easily see the entry of Jesus and his disciples into Jerusalem as triumphal, even though the city itself took little notice. Faith is the key to this seemingly insignificant event's meaning for history.75

Boff's concentration upon the death of Jesus is not concerned with establishing the historicity of the paschal events, he does concur with the results of such exegetes as Eduard Lohse, Josef Blinzler, and Pierre Benoit regarding what is probably historical and what is the work of the primitve community; however, he does not re-state their arguments. That enterprise is secondary to the question of the meaning of Jesus' death, which has several aspects. The first is the meaning for Jesus himself. Boff goes to great lengths to show that Jesus did not actively seek death; it was forced upon him.76 His acceptance was "not in a spirit of helpless resignation, or sovereign stoicism, but in human liberty, and hence as a person who rose above the exigencies of brute necessity."77 Following the Synoptic tradition interpreted in light of modern scholarship, Boff believes that Jesus gradually came to an awareness of his end. He maintains that "it was only on the cross that Jesus realized that his end was at hand--that he was really going to die."78 At that moment Jesus gave his life to the God he called "Abba". At that moment Jesus reached the apex of his being-for-others. The meaning of Jesus' death is consistent with the meaning of his life: "more justice, more love, more respect for the rights of the oppressed, and more liberty for God."79

The second aspect is the understanding of Jesus' death by the early church. This process has several stages. The first stage was a simple one: Jesus suffered the death that usually awaited a prophet of God. The second stage took this a step further. Many believed Jesus to be the Messiah, but the Messiah was expected to be gloriously victorious, not tortured and crucified; but this seemingly absurd death was only an appearance. God had not abandoned Jesus at his death. God raised Jesus from the dead because Jesus *had done* what God required: remained faithful to God's will to redeem humanity. The next stage emerged from the Jewish diaspora. With no Temple and no sacrifice, the Jews developed a theology of vicarious expiation of sin by the death of an innocent person. This theological atmosphere made it possible for diaspora Jewish Christians to "discover" the christological nature of Isaiah 53. The penultimate stage is found with Paul. To combat the enthusiasm that his preaching of the resurrection had inadvertently caused, he developed a theology of the cross. Over against the likes of the "super apostles," Paul shows that the "goodness" of the world, that is, the wisdom of the Greeks and the Law of the Jews, cannot save. In a world locked in slavery to sin and egoism, only one who gave himself for others can save. It is by the cross, the ultimate example of self-giving for others, that one can attain the joy of theresurrection. The final stage is found in the book of Hebrews. Jesus' death was a sacrifice to end all sacrifices. It opened up the age of the cosmic Christ, who continually intercedes before God on behalf of humanity.80

The third aspect consists of the way Jesus' death has been interpreted in the history of theology. This has taken one of three general forms: expiatory sacrifice, ransom from Satan, or vicarious satisfaction. The content, criticisms, and values of these models are well known and need not be discussed here. Boff's purpose in criticizing them is two-fold. First, he underscores their contextuality. He contends that this is natural, and that construction of new models is a valid enterprise. Second, he shows how they may impact upon a new cultural model, such as Jesus Christ Liberator. This model attempts, like the traditional ones, to say that:

> in [Jesus] the most radical anthropological structures, the locus of convergence of all our longings for oneness, reconciliation, communion, liberation, and intimacy with the Mystery that permeates our existence, spring into full bloom, achieve their maximal realization.[81]

The final aspect is the meaning of Jesus' death today. Theology in the modern period finds itself faced with "radical evil," an "antihistory . . . of evil, suffering, violence, and crime of immense dimensions";[82] in short, voluntary evil. On the one hand, there is a sense of justice when one suffers because of the evil one does. On the other hand, there is the suffering and death of the innocent, the ones who have striven for a more humane world. In light of this suffering, the phenomenon of various theologies of the cross have developed.

Probably the best known example of this theology is Jürgen Moltmann's, *The Crucified God*. Boff has serious misgivings about this view of the cross. For him, there can be no talk of a "revolt of God against God," of God's being both the object and subject of death. If this were true, there would be only one actor in the passion: God. All others merely follow the script given them; human freedom is an illusion. The consequences of such a one-actor drama is disastrous: "If suffering is an expression of God's very essence, if God hates, if God crucifies, then there is no salvation for us."[83]

This dialogue with Moltmann crystallizes what is the central problem of Jesus' death for Boff: meaningful suffering versus absurd suffering. The problem of suffering is intensified when it is the direct result of one's service to the kingdom of God, as it was for Jesus. In light of this service, what is the meaning of Christ's death? When is suffering not absurd? For Boff, suffering and death have meaning when they are endured for a just cause which "pursues the rights of the exploited against the legality of a distorted civil order."[84] One embarks on such a project believing that solidarity with the oppressed is the way to live out kingdom citizenship. Such a lifestyle mirrors that of Jesus. His pro-existence was "an attempt to overcome all conflicts in his own existence, and a realization of this goal."[85]

Jesus' Resurrection: Realization
  of Utopia

Faith in God, hope in God's future, and mirroring Jesus' comportment--all give meaning to suffering. They are means by which glimpses of the kingdom may be seen; therefore, they are incomplete in and of themselves. They point to something greater and all-encompassing. They reflect what Boff calls the "ultimate meaning of the death of Christ": the resurrection.[86] This event is the linch pin of Boff's Christology. All that has been said finds its full elucidation here. All that will follow flows from this event. Without the resurrection, Christian faith would be meaningless.

For Boff:

> Resurrection means the complete and definitive enthronement of human reality, spirit and body together, in the atmosphere of the divine. In other words, resurrection is complete hominization and liberation.[87]

Death is not the last word God pronounces over Jesus or humanity. With the resurrection, God revealed Jesus to his disciples "as one who while conserving his identity as Jesus of Nazareth manifested himself as totally transfigured and fully realized in his human and divine possibilities."[88] The experience of Jesus' resurrection was life changing for the disciples. They were given a new horizon for interpreting history.

The first impact that the resurrection had upon the primitive community was to "rehabilitate" Jesus before the world.[89] Boff's choice of "rehabilitate" is unsettling at first for it evokes images of prison inmates making license plates. But further contemplation reveals its appropriateness. Jesus' death by crucifixion had marked him as one abandoned by God, of no use to God. This image changed with his rising from the dead. Jesus had once again become useful and productive to God. Liberation from sin and death, and their specific manifestations in life, is what he now accomplishes. For Boff, this means the resurrection has "protest value" because "the one who was raised up is the one who was crucified. The liberator is the suffering servant, the oppressed one."[90] Negatively, it protests against the "justice" and the "law and order" that condemned Jesus to death. Positively, it gives meaning to the seemingly meaningless death experienced by those who advocate truth and justice.[91]

The disciples were also enabled to see the crucifixion in a multifaceted soteriological light. According to the tradition of "Q," even though Jesus suffered the fate of a prophet, God exalted him and constituted him "Son of Man." Another early source said Jesus died "to fulfill the Scriptures." The Palestinian community expanded this by saying Jesus' death was an extreme form of service.[92] Paul viewed Jesus' death as the end of the Law because Jesus took upon himself the curse of the Law. The common denominator among these views is that Jesus did not die because of his own sins and guilt, but because of the wickedness of human beings. Thus, Jesus:

> took on himself this perverted condition . . . . so that all might partake of the life that manifested itself in the resurrection: eternal life in communion with God, with others, and with the cosmos.[93]

Boff also makes the interesting claim that Jesus' death and resurrection "give origin to the Church." How this came about is not clear. The rejection of

Jesus by the Jews thwarted God's cosmic manifestation of the kingdom. So God realized it in Jesus. This specific realization opened a path "for a church with the same mission and message as Christ: little by little to announce and bring about the kingdom of God among human beings."[94] This implies that the cosmic Christ chooses not to reveal himself directly; he works through mediations. As Teilhard de Chardin has said, the church is "the central axis of universal convergence and precise point of encounter that emerges between the universe and the Omega point."[95] Because of the church's explicit historical linkage to Jesus Christ, it becomes the place where the cosmic Christ is most present in the world, continuing the mission of Jesus of Nazareth.

The fourth aspect of the resurrection is the answer to the most poignant of human questions: "What is to happen to humankind?" This question reflects the desire and the hope for realization of the self in spite of all the factors that inhibit this process. This hope gives rise to all sorts of utopias that promise the realization of the potentialities of human existence. For Boff:

> The resurrection of Jesus seeks to be this utopia realized within the world, because resurrection signifies an eschatologization of human reality, an introduction of the human person, body and soul, into the kingdom of God.[96]

Utopia no longer exists for the Christian. All the hopes and dreams that once constituted utopia are now "topia": the resurrected Jesus.

Therefore, the future of humankind is the present of the resurrected Jesus. Boff resorts here to the Pauline language of "spiritual body." For him, "body" refers to the capacity for communication, for relating to others. It is the corporal-spiritual identity referred to when one says "I."[97] In other words, "body" is both the means by which communication occurs and the content of that communication. In a sphere governed by time and space, relationships are accomplished through physical being. But the resurrection transforms this type of being into a spiritual existence where time and space have no meaning. This means that:

> humanity is unhindered and what erupts is (if to eternal life) the perfect and adequately complete spirit-body-world, without the spatial-temporal limitations of the history of sin.[98]

At that time, everyone will receive the body (the means for communication) that they deserve, that is, one which corresponds to, and fully expresses, their corporal-spiritual identity.[99]

Thus, there is a direct relationship between life before and after resurrection. As Boff says:

> At the time of death the human being, the unity of body-soul, will enter into a total and definitive realization of that which was sown on earth: resurrection for life or death. The cadaver can stay behind and be handed over to corruption; our true body, personalized by "I" . . . will participate in eternal life.[100]

It is at this point that what was confusing becomes even moreso: How does "resurrection for life or death" mesh with "participate in eternal life"? The latter phrase is definitely positive while the former is only partly so. Is Boff referring to dual destinies after resurrection? The first sentence just quoted seems to imply this. Or is he referring to the Rauschenbuschian idea that those who were once served (the oppressors) become the servants of those who once served (the oppressed)? Perhaps this is a question that does not concern Boff. Perhaps the answer lies in the grace-full work of the Cosmic Christ.[101] At any rate, Boff's basic point is that since God is making the new out of the old, Christians should be concerned with the world in which they live. He puts it this way: "In Jesus, resurrection means the victory of life, the victory of the rights of the oppressed, the victory of justice for the weak."[102] This is something that must not be lost in the shuffle of the questions just raised.

The path Boff has traveled to arrive at this understanding of Jesus' resurrection is a familiar one. First, he goes to Scripture and finds two pieces of evidence: the empty sepulcher and the "apparitions," that is, the appearances of Jesus. These stories circulated separately for years before they were finally, and roughly, compressed into one. All the accounts agree that the women found the tomb empty; but instead of inspiring faith, it evoked fear. Boff says it well when he states, "The empty tomb is a sign which speaks to all and leads to reflection on the possibility of faith."[103] The "apparitions" are the origin of faith in the resurrection of Jesus, for they removed the ambiguity surrounding the empty tomb. Second, the appearances are a presence similar and dissimilar to what Jesus had known before.[104] That is to say, he was recognizable within the bounds of time and space, but he was not confined to those bounds. Thus, Boff's use of the Pauline category of spiritual body is an attempt to state how the risen One is also the One who was crucified.

The Christological Process

The development of Christology is the historical and ongoing answer to the question, "Who is Jesus and what does he signify for human existence?" This process began during Jesus' lifetime: people were astonished at him because of the vitality of his life and teaching. This astonishment led to a negative and a positive Christology, albeit indirectly. The former was articulated by Jesus' enemies scandalized by his liberating attitudes towards sinners and the Law. The latter came from those who saw something new in Jesus that they had not seen or heard from any other rabbi.[105]

Boff raises the question of why Jesus did not use any of the messianic or apocalyptic titles available to him to express his growing awareness of his relationship to God's kingdom. This question is even more intriguing in light of the fact that Jesus used apocalypticism to communicate his message of the kingdom. Part of the answer is that a growing awareness of self means changes in attitudes and understanding. But Boff locates the primary reason in the fact that "Jesus was far too simple, sovereign, and attached to the lowly classes and the socially disqualified" to attribute such titles to himself.[106] In other words, they would have been detrimental to the new solidarity Jesus was inaugurating.

The New Testament Process

The resurrection changed this situation dramatically. The shift from an indirect to direct Christology began a process that seeks "to situate Jesus within the totality of human life as it is lived and understood by human beings within history."[107] This process began in the Palestinian Jewish Christian communities and their appropriation of eschatological and apocalyptic titles. Specifically, Jesus was interpreted as having been proclaimed by God to be the Son of God by the resurrection. The Jewish Christian communities of the diaspora continued this process by their calling Jesus "Lord," that is, Lord of the whole cosmos and of all humanity. This appellation does not yet refer to divinity. Gentile Christians carried the process forward as they sought to understand Jesus in a Hellenistic world. For them, Jesus was the Savior, that is, the one who liberates humanity and the cosmos. "Son of God" was taken from its original juridical context and was made physical: Jesus was ontologically the Son of God. If Son, then he was pre-existent with God and, thus, equal with God. The constant factor in this process is that "everything important and essential to human life and history was attributed to Christ, including the most sublime reality that can possibly exist, God."[108]

This process, ending with divinity, does not seek to eliminate the humanity of Jesus. Rather, it seeks to highlight it. As Boff says, "it is not the titles that create his authority; rather, his authority gave origin to the titles."[109] The disciples meditated upon the life, death, and resurrection of Jesus before they called him God. Thus, they began from below and reached the highest point possible. This process opened new situations and new questions regarding the birth of Jesus.

The basic question that the birth narratives answer is this: "When did God institute Jesus as Savior?" The oldest preaching pointed to his death and resurrection. Mark moved it back to his baptism. Matthew moved it back further to his birth. Luke concurred with this, but added that all of history had been progressing toward him. Finally, John said that Jesus was the Son of God before creation. Obviously, these narratives are the result of a well-thought-out theology that "through graphic, theological narrations . . . is an announcement of Jesus of Nazareth, *who he is* and *what he is*, for the community of faith in about the years A.D. 80-90."[110]

The facts, according to critical Catholic exegesis, are: the engagement of Mary and Joseph; Davidic descendency through Joseph; the name "Jesus"; his virgin birth; and Nazareth as his home. Matthew and Luke worked with these facts to show that in this child:

> lay hidden the secret meaning of all history since the creation of the first being and that in him all the prophecies and human hopes for liberation and the fullness of God were realized.[111]

The rest of the birth narratives--the genealogies, the virgin birth, the place of Bethlehem and Nazareth, parallels with John the Baptist and Moses, the shepherds and the Magi-- function to uphold this claim.112

Such a demythologizing of the birth narratives opens the door for modern Christians to see "their true religio-anthropological significance": "Today a liberator has been born to you, he is Christ the Lord" (Lk. 2:11). As Boff points out:

> from the very beginning, Jesus appears among the oppressed. . . . The social and economic poverty of Jesus' land is emphasized in Jesus' identification with the poor and downtrodden.113

For the early church, humiliation characterized Jesus' messiahship. All who are oppressed may gain strength from the knowledge that the messiah is one of them. This identification with the downtrodden frees them for a new solidarity.114 But, in order to plumb the depths of this insight, Christians today are forced to use myths and symbols. These forms of communication reach a deeper level than do brute facts.115 So continue to speak of these elements of the Christmas story, Boff says, for "they make us plunge into the depths of a reality where we begin to perceive the divine and human transparency in the most banal things as well as the meaning of life."116

Chalcedon

The New Testament process points to the importance of christological dogmas. They provide a starting point for speaking about the impact Jesus had during his life and upon those who hear him proclaimed today. But the recitation of ancient dogmas does not ensure orthodoxy. As Boff says: "We are required to live the mystery that the formulas contain and always try to express it anew within our language and for our own times."117 Abstract analysis of "God" and "human nature" does not facilitate this, as if one already knew what these terms signified. Theologians need to remember that "it was in a man that the primitive church discovered God; and it was in God that we came to know the true nature and destiny of human beings."118 To do Christology, one must begin with Jesus as the starting point. "Only then," says Boff, "after being inserted into his life, can theologians perceive [Jesus'] meaning and begin to see God in the human being and the human being in God."119

The history of theology reveals many attempts to do this, acccompanied by many errors and deviations; one may say too much or too little. To speak with Jesus as the starting point means overstressing neither his humanity nor divinity. Orthodoxy is found in holding in tension the human and divine natures in Jesus. The theological battles and the resulting Ecumenical Councils are well known and need not be discussed here. Suffice it to say, there are four basic imbalances in the history of Christology. The first is the tendency to exalt the divine nature over the human. The second is the lifting up of the human nature to the detriment of the divine. Another tendency is to have so radical a union that one nature absorbs the other. The final tendency is the co-existence of two complete persons in one body. All four of these imbalances derive from a static ontology of human and divine natures. In any case, one either falls into monophysitism (emphasizing the unity with God) or Nestorianism (postulating a duality of persons in Jesus).120 Thus, the preservation of orthodoxy depends upon two elements: 1) one must begin with Jesus of Nazareth; and 2) a dynamic understanding of divine and human nature must be present. Anything less is heresy.

With this in mind, Boff turns his attention to the church's christological watershed: the Council of Chalcedon in 451 C.E. The council's statement was a composite of the best of the Alexandrian and Antiochene schools of thought. With Alexandria, it taught a unity of person in Jesus, but not of natures. With Antioch, it stressed the duality of natures, but not of persons. The text does not explain how two natures cooperate to form one person; it only sets forth the basic criteria for talking about the mystery of Jesus Christ; that is to say, "the complete humanity and the true divinity of Jesus ought to be simultaneously maintained without dividing his fundamental unity."[121]

The council used the language of its day to strike this delicate balance. "Nature" referred to "all that perfects the human being and the divine being";[122] it is synonymous with essence or substance. "Person" seeks to express the principle of unity in being, that which makes anything one; "it is a way or manner of existing."[123] For the council, the one person of the Logos is the bearer of the two natures. Jesus' human nature was not annihilated by this assumption; rather, it was totally realized, not in itself, but in the divine person. In other words, the basis of life for the man-Jesus was not himself but God.[124]

Boff's criticism of the council's statement is multifaceted. First, he points out that today "nature" is understood in a dynamic fashion as the result of a long biological and cultural evolutionary process. "Person" is this nature as it is realized in its relationship to, and communion with, the totality of reality. Second, the council's static understanding of nature does not take into account the changes in Jesus as portrayed in the Synoptics. Third, it does not perceive the transformation of Jesus in the resurrection, that is, the transition from physical body to spiritual body. Fourth, by beginning with the incarnation, the council makes the kenosis of God in Jesus difficult to comprehend. Fifth, there is the lack of a universal, cosmic perspective; the council was concerned solely with human salvation. Finally, the affirmation of two natures runs the risk of placing God and humanity on the same level.[125]

How, then, does Boff reconstruct the Chalcedonian affirmation that Jesus is truly human and truly divine? Methodologically, he turns to Jesus of Nazareth. Boff contends that God, divinity, humanity, person, and nature can be understood rightly only from that vantage point.

For Boff, Jesus lived his life open to others, accepting them, loving them (often with a love that included harsh words), teaching them, and remaining faithful to all, even in death. Empty of himself, he could be filled by others. The same may be said of his relationship with God. Contrary to Chalcedon, Jesus did not possess a *hypostasis*, a subsistence which existed in himself and for himself.[126] Instead, he totally opened himself to God as other and was filled with the Other. Without this type of openness and giving, one cannot know oneself. As Boff says, "it is by going out of oneself that human beings remain profoundly within their own selves; it is by giving that one receives and possesses one's being."[127]

Therefore, Jesus was the human being *par excellence*, not because he defended to the end his "I," but because he surrendered and communicated his "I" to the other. From Jesus we learn what constitutes true human being: namely, openness to the world, others, and God. In an extended passage, Boff reveals Jesus as the human being who is God and the God who is human:

> The more human beings relate to others and go out of themselves, the more they grow and become human. The more they are in the other, the more they are in themselves and become themselves. The more Jesus existed in God, the more God resided in him. The more the man-Jesus dwelled in God, the more he was divinized. The more God existed in Jesus, the more God was humanized. The man-Jesus was in God in such a way that they became identified; God made himself human so that the human could become God.[128]

Consistency in logic and methodology requires a different solution from the one Boff has given. Interestingly enough, Boff himself refers to such an answer. He points to Piet Schoonenberg's, *The Christ*, as a Christology similar to his own, that is, one which begins with Jesus' humanity and ends with his divinity. Schoonenberg states that the humanity of Jesus "is a self-evident presupposition of all christology [*sic*], especially biblical theology."[129] With this in mind, Schoonenberg goes on to say:

> Now not the human but the divine nature in Christ is enhypostatic, with the provisio, moreover, that this is valid inasmuch as we do not know the person of the Word outside the man Jesus. However, it is primarily not the human nature which is enhypostatic in the divine person, but the divine nature in the human person.[130]

This view allows one to affirm both the humanity and divinity of Jesus, and that his humanity reveals his divinity.

By working this way (from below), Boff has reversed the logic of Chalcedon. Instead of beginning with the Incarnation, he ends there. Therefore, God's becoming should not be seen only as God's participation in the human condition; it should also be viewed in light of the resurrection, when all that had been hidden in Jesus was fully realized: "a universal and maximum openness to all cosmic, human, and divine reality."[131]

With Jesus as the starting point, a new understanding of human being is reached. If Jesus actually was a human being, then what was said of him must in some way be said of all persons. The Franciscans have long held the belief that human beings are capable of the Infinite. Love makes this possible. Through love, people can open themselves to others and God, become empty of self, and be filled by others and God. Even in sin and alienation, this oneness can be achieved to some degree. A future of more fulfillment may be anticipated until people achieve their own resurrection. Thus, Boff contends that "human being" ought to be interpreted in light of its future rather than in terms of its biological past. Incarnation is not only about Jesus; it is also about everyone. The Incarnation reveals the nature of God, who human beings are, and what their destiny is.[132]

One aspect of Jesus Christ has not been addressed: the sinlessness of Jesus. If one follows the reasoning of Chalcedon, sinlessness is a fore-gone conclusion: one begins with the incarnation of the second person of the Trinity, and by definition, God cannot sin. This is further guaranteed by the virgin birth. Since Boff reverses this reasoning and ends with the incarnation, the question of sinlessness is raised again.

Boff takes seriously Luke's statement that Jesus "increased in wisdom and in stature, and in favor with God and man" (Lk. 2:52). He contends that this statement is essential to understanding Jesus' sinlessness. In other words, incarnation is a dynamic, life-long process. In every phase of his life, God assumed:

> the human concrete nature of Jesus according to how this manifested itself and developed. The inverse is also true: The human nature of Jesus revealed the divinity according to how it increased and matured.[133]

The highs and lows of human life presented Jesus with the opportunity to plumb the depths of human and divine nature. With the crucifixion and resurrection, the ultimate in divine-human communication and self-giving occurred. In this two-sided event "matter and spirit, and God, arrive at an unspeakable unity and a full interpenetration."[134] In other words, Jesus' divinity is revealed through his humanity. This enables Boff to say that:

> because Jesus was emptied of his own self and completely centered in God, he was without sin; because he persevered in this fundamental attitude not only did he not sin but he could not sin.[135]

What about original sin? If Jesus was truly human, did he not participate:

> in the schizophrenia of our historical existence which makes us . . . incapable of decentering ourselves radically [and] ontologically distorts us even in our ultimate biological roots and place us in a bent position before God?[136]

Boff answers no, Jesus assumed only "the history of human sin." Here Boff borrows the Jungian idea that everyone carries in the unconscious the entire history of human evolution. If this is true, in the incarnation (as process) "the Word, humanizing itself, assumed all this reality contained in the collective and personal human psyche, both positive and negative, thereby touching all humanity."[137] Jesus overcame the negative aspects by the power of the Holy Spirit. The positive aspects "were activated, allowing the human being who is really image and likeness of God to emerge."[138]

The Christological Process Today

This discussion reveals that Boff sees Christology as a process in which Christians have an active role--a process that did not stop with Chalcedon, but continues today. Both the past and the future impact how Christology is done today. The past sets up the parameters within which Christology takes place. The future gives it its shape. Without the future, the past would degenerate into legalism; without the past, the future would be mere speculation. The future is so important to Boff because "the resurrection opened up a new dimension of reality and traced a new horizon of comprehension."139 This is not to be understood as merely hoping that everything will turn out all right in the end. It is hope of a specific kind; it has a name: the resurrected Jesus.

One reason that Boff writes with such hope is the cosmic Christ, which is his term for the risen Lord. This mode of being came about because, with the resurrection, "Christ penetrated [the world] in a more profound manner and is now present in all reality in the same way God is present in all things."140 Jesus is no longer bound by time and space. The man-Jesus is now absolutely open to the God Jesus, thereby completely realizing Jesus' capacity for communion and communication with the cosmos. Reflection upon this event led the early church to begin a cosmic and transcendental Christology: All reality converges on Christ; he is the fullness of time and of all things; he created all things, and in him all things exist and consist.141 Simply put, "cosmic Christology . . . basically professes that Christ is the beginning, the middle, and the end of God's paths and the measure of all things."142

The cosmic Christ has no barriers to his activities. The renewed interest in space exploration raises again the question of life on other planets. Even though the future ultimately holds the answer to this question, Boff believes the church should have some sort of response, however preliminary. This response is based upon the work of the cosmic Christ. These lifeforms, while strangers to humans, are not so to Christ, for he created them. He knows them as well as he does humanity. With their needs in mind, the cosmic Christ may be incarnated according to "the spiritual and evolutionary conditions of [these] beings."143

Temporally speaking, the cosmic Christ is at work in all people. For Boff, this means "each person is actually a brother or sister to Jesus and in some way participates in his reality."144 This familial relationship is evidenced whenever one loves and accepts the other, which reveals the mystery of personhood, that is, that there is more to people than their physical being and its concretizations in word and deed. The mystery of personhood evokes the mystery of God, for humanity is made in the image and likeness of God; therefore, there is more to God than meets the eye.145

The negative side of this, rejection of the other, evokes harsh words from Boff: "Whoever rejects his brother or sister rejects Christ himself, because whoever rejects the image and likeness of God and Christ rejects God and Christ himself."146 Boff goes on to say: "Without the sacrament of brother and sister no one can be saved."147 This is the reason that liberation theology emphasizes the relationships between people here and now. The way people relate to one another reveals their relationship to God. Non-loving actions and attitudes toward others reflects an un-loving attitude toward God.

Therefore, whoever does not love and accept the other is not a follower of Jesus. It does not matter whether or not one confesses "Jesus is Lord." How one lives reveals one's faith or lack of faith. It is apparent that Boff utilizes a broad definition of "Christian" when dealing with the workings of the cosmic Christ. For Boff:

> Wherever people seek the good, justice, humanitarian love, solidarity, communion, and understanding between people, wherever they dedicate themselves to overcoming their own egoism, making this world more human and fraternal, and opening themselves to the normative Transcendent for their lives, there we can say, with all certainty, that the resurrected one is present, because the cause for which he lived, suffered, was tried and executed is being carried forward.[148]

Differences in culture, tradition, history, and world-view will result in different responses to the leadership of the cosmic Christ. This does not mean that every aspect of a given religion is legitimized, for all human activities contain errors and misinterpretations. Each religion, however, "ought to keep itself open, criticize itself, and develop an even more adequate response to God's proposal."[149]

While the cosmic Christ works incognito in many peoples and religions, he wears the name Jesus when working in those who confess themselves as Christians. These people differ from "anonymous Christians" in that they consciously attempt to imitate Jesus. Boff's *imitatio Christi* means:

> trying to act in our existential situation in the same way Christ acted in his situation. . . . It means having the same attitude and the same spirit as Jesus, incarnating it in our concrete situation, which is different from that of Jesus.[150]

On the positive side, this means being with people and persevering to the end in faith and love and all that is good in humanity. On the negative side, it means being critical of anything that dehumanizes people or inhibits freedom for God and others.[151]

Lest this be misinterpreted in an individualistic way, Boff points out that the same Christ who is present in all who carry his cause forward finds his highest level of historical concretion in the church, the community of faith. "Because of its strict and unbroken link with Jesus Christ whom it preaches, preserves, and lives in its sacraments and ministries, and to whose criticism it subjects itself," the church should be seen as a "special institutional articulation of Christianity."[152] This link does not legitimize every aspect of the life or activity of the Church, for much of its history is decidedly un-Christlike; but in its worship, liturgy, preaching, gestures, and symbols it attempts to make present the resurrected Jesus.[153]

To say that the Church is a "special institutional articulation of Christianity" does not detract from the "religious and salvific value" of other religions. They are articulations of Christianity, also; therefore, there needs to be a dialogue between the two. Other religions should welcome the Church's criticism for it will broaden their horizons and help them "grow to an ever more adequate openness to God's proposal as manifested in Jesus Christ."[154] Likewise, the Church should be open to criticism from other religions, for they may have perfected certain "facets and dimensions of religious experience" the Church has not. This dialogue will allow the Church to become truly universal "because it will also know how to see and capture the reality of God and Christ outside its own articulation and outside the sociological limits of its own reality."[155]

In other words, theological language is not the only legitimate way to describe God's work in the world. Boff spends considerable time delving into the "elements of a Christology in secular language." While he does not name these "languages," it is possible to do so. If one uses evolutionary language, one could speak of Christ as the Omega Point of history. Sociological language interprets Christ as the Divine Milieu of life. A kinship with Christ the Liberator allows one to use the language of politics in Christology. Psychology has long been used in theology, albeit in a translated form; now, its original form is sufficient. The language of human experience, of day-to-day life, reveals the relevance of Christ for today's relationships. Even specifically theological language is necessary for life in a global village.[156]

There is, then, a christic structure to reality. Boff has arrived at this conclusion via his methodology. He began with the story of Jesus of Nazareth, examined the early church's writings about him, and ended with Jesus Christ pre-existent, co-existent, and one with God from all eternity. Christ, then, has been at work in the world since the beginning of creation. Following a Teilhardian evolutionary schema, Boff states that Christ began the process of cosmogenesis. Then, working in, with, and through the stuff of creation, Christ effected the beginning of life: biogenesis. Through millions of years of evolution, anthropogenesis was begun. Finally, "in the fullness of time," Christogenesis, the incarnation of God in Jesus of Nazareth, occurred. Jesus of Nazareth, the Christ of God, is the definitive realization of this christic structure. With the resurrection, the humanity and divinity of Jesus achieved absolute openness and communion, constituting a new type of existence: a spiritual body totally at one with God and the cosmos. On this basis, Boff writes:

> from all of this follows that creation has, in its most intimate being, christic traces, mirroring in myriads of different facets the same face and form as the cosmic body of Christ.[157]

In other words, just as the cosmic Christ touches all of reality, so all of reality reveals that touch in its own unique way.

Christology in Boff's Theology

The presence of Boff's Christology in his theology is largely a matter of interpretation. Occasionally, he will make explicit reference to some aspect of Christology and how it relates to his subject matter. Usually, however, one has the feeling of having read this or that idea before; therefore, what follows is this writer's interpretation of two aspects of Boff's theology: the church and the world. This may seem rather selective, but it will provide insights into the way Boff's Christology affects his thoughts on the other theological subjects.

Boff's major writings on the Church are *Ecclesiogenesis*[158] and *Church: Charism and Power*.[159] The former is an apology for the base ecclesial communities that have spread throughout Latin America, while the latter addresses the church as institution. The base ecclesial communities are a new form of church "rotating on the axis of the word and the laity."[160] Life in the base communities:

> is characterized by the absence of alienating structures, by direct relationships, by reciprocity, by a deep communion, by mutual assistance, by communality of gospel ideals, [and] by equality among members.[161]

To be sure, conflicts do arise, but great effort is made to overcome them. Such a life is an attempt to live out Jesus' praxis of love, hope, and humanization. Participation in a base community allows the people to enter into a new solidarity, to live a lifestyle of being-for-others, and to incarnate Jesus' preferential option for the poor.[162]

The base communities allow Christians a chance to claim their own sphere of activity within the universal scope of the cosmic Christ. They may work with the institutional Church, with churches outside of Roman Catholicism, or with groups that call for love and justice without a conscious acknowledgement of Jesus Christ.[163] Thus, the base communities are concerned with all things and all people, thereby incarnating the universal salvific will of God in Jesus Christ. In doing so, they:

> prove that it is possible to be Christian without being conservative, that one can be a person of faith while at the same time committed to society and its future, that one can hope in eternity without losing one's foothold in the struggle for a better tomorrow.[164]

This ability prevents a ghettoization of the church and gives occasion for celebration over any progress that is made for love and justice.

This is not to say that living for justice, mercy, and equality is easy. Boff made it clear that following Jesus often results in violence, torture, and death. In his book on the stations of the cross, Boff telescopes the life and praxis of Jesus into his last days. But the experience of Jesus is only part of the story of the stations. The stations also apply to anyone who follows Jesus in a world characterized by hate and injustice.[165]

Boff goes to great lengths to say that the base ecclesial communities are not a new Church. He plainly says that "there is no change in the ongoing coexistence of one aspect that is more static, institutional, and permanent with another that is more dynamic, charismatic, and vital."[166] The base communities represent a reinvention of the Church from the bottom up. The laity, as the People of God, is fundamental; the hierarchical structure follows. This view of the church parallels Jesus' primary ministry to the bottom of society: the poor, tax collectors, prostitutes, and sinners.[167]

Boff's criticism of the hierarchical model of the Church (God-Christ-Apostles-Bishops-Priests-Laity) reflects Jesus' position vis-à-vis the Law. If it brings the people and God together, it is good. If it does not, it must be changed. For Boff, the hierarchical model needs changing. He contends that "*the hierarchy has the sacramental function of organizing and serving a reality that it has not created but discovered, and within which it finds itself.*"[168] The reason for this is simple: Within the Church, "there is not one group of rulers and another group of those who are ruled; there is one group of faith."[169] Therefore, the laity should be allowed to participate in the decision-making process of the Church, allowing them to become active participants in their own history. Since Christ met people where they were, allowing them to define themselves, the Church of Christ cannot do otherwise.[170]

If the Church is reinvented, it follows that the mission of the Church is also altered. Evangelization of the world "is not a matter . . . of *transplanting* the church deductively, but of *implanting* the church inductively."[171] This is the way the church opens itself to the workings of the cosmic Christ outside its own boundaries without losing its identity as the Church. When the Church comes into contact with other religions, it should state unequivocally its profession of faith in Jesus Christ as the definitive self-revelation of God. As the Church dialogues with these religions, it should expect to find religious expressions of love, justice, and mercy, which are nothing but the workings of the cosmic Christ, albeit incognito. When it does, the Church should purify these acts of their superstition and magic, and accept them as indigenous expressions of faith.[172]

The experience of the cosmic Christ in the world today is the subject of Boff's *Liberating Grace*.[173] For Boff, "grace is not a quality of God . . . . he is grace."[174] That is to say, grace is God's presence in the world, God's giving of Godself to the world. Grace is openness, dialogue, and communion. Grace is also historical. In the Old Testament, it was evident in events such as the Exodus and the election of Israel. In the New Testament, grace is the story of Jesus Christ. In short, grace must be an experience within time and space, that is, history.[175]

Then grace fell into the hands of theologians; it became a dogma instead of an experience. This dogma was written by priests and religious, people removed from the fabric of everyday life. Boff contends that "it was the limited outlook of a clerical, ghetto-minded theology that restricted the life of grace and divine filiation solely to Christians."[176] In other words, the experience of grace outside the church was lost; it became the sole property of the hierarchy.[177]

With this in mind, attention may be turned to the ways grace is experienced in the world. Boff contends that the secularity of the world must be taken seriously; science and technology define the world. This should not be an insurmountable obstacle or a sign of "dis-grace" to the Christian. To the eyes of faith, "everything is grace because everything is referred back to him, sustained and supported ontologically by him."[178] This universal sustenance and support implies that grace is "given in mediations, negotiations, relations, and social structures."[179] Thus, faith can see God at work (grace) humanizing the world through (mediated by) human action.

What are some of the events and actions that Boff contends mediate grace in the world today? Actions such as refraining from self-justification, and self-denial for a good cause, reflect an ability to transcend the moment. The mere fact of existence is a gift, for nothing created is necessary. The reality of love, friendship, and communion with others make it moreso. Authentic human encounters in which two people open themselves to each other is an experience of grace. In fact, anywhere love, openness, and mutuality occur is grace, and is experienced as such by those who live them out. Boff gives many more examples, most of them being things that people take for granted.[180] But they are all the work of the cosmic Christ continuing the incarnation of Jesus of Nazareth today. They call for love of neighbor, love of God, mercy, and justice. They foreshadow the realization of the utopia of the kingdom of God, when there will be total and open communion of human beings with themselves, others, and God.

Conclusion

The purpose of this chapter is to provide an analytic exposition of Boff's Christology. As such, it is written from a sympathetic point of view. Even so, some inconsistencies are present. One concerns Boff's treatment of the sinlessness of Jesus vis-à-vis original sin. In this writer's opinion, Boff has gone to a lot of trouble for nothing. Evidently he has accepted the traditional view of original sin (with the variation of not attributing original sin to Adam and Eve): one person committed an act that twisted and stained everyone else. Such a view does not fit in with the evolutionary view of human development that Boff has advocated. Nor does it follow his own methodology, for it seems to be more the result of an abstract definition of original sin rather than a conclusion gleaned from an examination of the life of Jesus. This criticism does not imply that the concept of original sin has no place in Christology. But a redefinition seems necessary in light of Boff's methodology.

Based upon what Boff has said concerning the sinlessness of Jesus, the following may serve as an understanding of original sin consistent with the life of Jesus. Proceeding from the resurrection, one may conclude that Jesus did not sin. Moreover, he did not sin because he chose not to sin (a paraphrase of Jesus' desire to do only the will of God). Because Jesus was truly human and was also without sin, it may be concluded that sinfulness is not innately human. But sin exists. Therefore, at some point in the distant past of human evolution someone committed the original (first) sin. The door was opened for Sin to enter the world and wreak its havoc. Due to its power, Sin quickly permeated the cosmos. The frailty of the evolving human will was not strong enough to withstand Sin's tide and humanity fell under its sway (note that Sin entered the world and not humanity's biological evolution). But "in the fullness of time" there appeared a person who could stand against Sin: Jesus of Nazareth. In him God proleptically effected the defeat of Sin.

To be sure, many gaps are present in this view of original sin. It is merely a sketch, not a fully developed portrait. But this is true of any view of original sin. Anytime one deals with prehistory, the lack of concrete data leads to conjectures and educated guesses. Still, this view is consistent with Boff's view of evolutionary reality, his presentation of Jesus as truly human, and of the sinlessness of Jesus. It also reflects Paul's statement that Sin entered the world through the action of one person and that Sin was defeated by the action of one person (Rom. 5:18).

The second area relates to Boff's analysis of Chalcedon. He has attempted to strike a delicate balance between his criticism and his reconstruction of Chalcedon, but he has not been very successful. On the one hand, he follows the traditional understanding that the person of the Logos is the bearer of two natures; human nature is *enhypostatic* within the divine. On the other hand, he builds a strong case for Jesus' humanity's revealing his divinity. The question arises: Can that which is borne (humanity) reveal its bearer (divinity)? This is possible if one begins with the Incarnation, with God's becoming human in order to effect human salvation; but this goes against Boff's methodology of starting with Jesus of Nazareth. It also contradicts his contention that Jesus' humanity reveals his divinity. As Boff said of Chalcedon, this makes the kenosis of God in Jesus incomprehensible. For this writer, the power and ability to reveal reside in the bearer and not in what is borne.

Notes

[1] Biographical information was gleaned from: Leonardo Boff, *Jesus Christ Liberator: A Critical Christology for Our Time*, trans. Patrick Hughes (Maryknoll: Orbis Books, 1978), cited hereafter as *Liberator*; *Liberating Grace*, trans. John Drury (Maryknoll: Orbis Books, 1979), cited hereafter as *Liberating Grace*; *Passion of Christ, Passion of the World: The Facts, Their Interpretation, and Their Meaning Yesterday and Today*, trans. Robert R. Barr (Maryknoll: Orbis Books, 1987), cited hereafter as *Passion*; Boff and Clodovis Boff, *Liberation Theology: From Dialogue to Confrontation*, trans. Robert R. Barr (San Francisco: Harper & Row, 1986), pp. 75-91; Deane William Ferm, *Third World Liberation Theologies: An Introductory Surve*: (Maryknoll: Orbis Books, 1986), p. 123; and Ferm, *Profiles in Liberation: 36 Portraits of Third World Theologians* (Mystic, Connecticut: Twenty-Third Publications, 1988), pp. 124-28.

[2] Boff, *Liberator*, p. xii.   [3] Ibid.

[4] Boff utilized the same methodology in *A Ressurreição de Cristo: A Nossa Ressurreição na Morte*, 3d ed. (Petrópolis, RJ: Editôra Vozes Ltda, 1974), pp. 19-40, cited hereafter as *Ressurreição* and *O Evangelho do Cristo Cósmico: A Realidade de um Mito, O Mito de uma Realidade* (Petrópolis, RJ: Editôra Vozes Ltda, 1971), pp. 63-91, cited hereafter as *Evangelho*.

[5] Boff, *Liberator*, pp. 12-15. Boff drinks deeply from the modern critical interpretation of Jesus. Historical criticism is essential to his portrayal of who Jesus was and how he understood his ministry. He almost constructs a "life of Jesus" as he attempts to show the relevance and meaning of Jesus for the final quarter of the twentieth century in Latin America. Finally, Boff goes to great lengths to reveal the continuity between Jesus of Nazareth and the Christ of faith.

[6] Ibid., pp. 20-21.   [7] Ibid., pp. 21-22.

[8]Boff, *Liberator*, pp. 25-28. Boff also referred to three other movements: Death of God theology, depth psychology, and the youth counterculture. While he was appreciative of the Christological concentration of the Death of God movement, he criticized its reductionism: Jesus' primary reference point was outside himself, in God (pp. 15-17). The primary contribution of depth psychology was its insistence that myth was a valid way for the collective unconscious of humanity to explain existence (pp. 22-24). Finally, the revival of religion in the counterculture of the late Sixties and early Seventies revealed the innate human longing for God that the cosmic Christ facilitates in his presence today (pp. 28-31).

[9]Ibid., p. 41.   [10]Ibid., pp. 38-39.   [11]Ibid., p. 39.   [12]Ibid., pp. 39-40.

[13]Ibid., p. 40.   [14]Ibid., p. 41.   [15]Ibid.   [16]Ibid., pp. 41-42.   [17]Ibid., p. 43.

[18]Ibid., p. 44.   [19]Ibid.   [20]Ibid.   [21]Ibid., pp. 44-45.   [22]Ibid., p. 45.   [23]Ibid.

[24]Ibid., p. 46.   [25]Ibid., pp. 46-47.   [26]Ibid., p. 269.   [27]Ibid., p. 270.

[28]Ibid., p. 272.

[29]To be sure, social analysis generally comes to mind first when one thinks of liberation theology. But now that its place in theology has been secured, its theologians have begun producing more "hermeneutical" works. For example, see Gustavo Gutiérrez, *We Drink from Our Own Wells: The Spiritual Journey of a People*, trans. Matthew J. O'Connell (Maryknoll: Orbis Books, 1984) and Boff, *Liberating Grace*.

[30]Boff, *Liberator*, pp. 49-50.   [31]Ibid., p. 52.   [32]Ibid., p. 53.   [33]Ibid., pp. 52-53.

[34]Ibid., p. 55.   [35]Ibid., p. 56.   [36]Ibid., pp. 56-57.   [37]Quoted by Boff, ibid., p. 57.

[38]Ibid.   [39]Ibid., p. 58.   [40]Ibid., p. 60.   [41]Ibid.   [42]Ibid., p. 65.

[43]Ibid., p. 68.   [44]Ibid., pp. 70-72.   [45]Ibid., p. 72.   [46]Ibid., pp. 72-75.

[47]Ibid., p. 76.   [48]See below, pp. 40-42.   [49]Ibid., p. 77.   [50]Ibid., p. 78.

[51]See below, p. 39.   [52]Ibid., pp. 80-81.   [53]Ibid., p. 81.   [54]Ibid., p. 83.

[55]Ibid., pp. 81-85.   [56]Ibid., pp. 90-91.   [57]Ibid., pp. 90-92.

[58]Ibid., p. 305, n. 11: Four Synoptic texts have Jesus using this word or a derivative. Boff said both Luke 17:6 and 10:20 lack a moral context and the former was an editorial revision of Mark 11:23. So was Matthew 21:23. Matthew 18:17 reflected the theology of the primitive church.

[59]Boff, *Liberator* p. 92.   [60]Ibid., p. 95.   [61]Ibid., p. 96.   [62]Ibid., pp. 95-96.

[63]Ibid., p. 98.

[64]Wolfhart Pannenberg, *Jesus--God and Man*, 2nd ed. trans. Lewis L. Wilkins and Duane A. Priebe (Philadelphia: Westminster Press, 1977), p. 48. Cited hereafter as *Jesus*. Cf. Boff, *Liberator*, pp. 117-18: "Everything seems to indicate that in the beginning the apostles did not see any salvific significance in the death of Christ. . . . Only after the resurrection did they decipher with growing clarity the meaning of death and resurrection as two scenes of the same salvific act."

[65]Pannenberg, *Jesus*, p. 49. Cf. Boff, *Liberator*, p. 121: "Jesus announced an absolute meaning to the world as a total liberation from all alienations that stigmatize human existence: from pain, from hatred, from sin, and finally from death as well."

[66]Boff, *Passion*, pp. 1-2.   [67]Ibid., pp. 4-6.   [68]Ibid., p. 13.   [69]Ibid., p. 17.

[70]Ibid., pp. 17-18. For a criticism of this point, see Wolfhart Pannenberg, "The Resurrection of Jesus and the Future of Mankind," trans M. B. Jackson in *The Cumberland Seminarian*, XIX (1981), 45.

[71]Boff, *Passion*, p. 18.   [72]Ibid., pp. 19-20.   [73]Ibid., pp. 20-21.   [74]Ibid., p. 24.

[75]See Ibid., pp. 26-31 for a discussion of these three examples. For similar conclusions on other paschal events, see pp. 31-43.

[76]Jesus was crucified as a blasphemer, a weak Messiah with no army, and abandoned by his closest followers, an idea anathema in a time of rampant nationalism (ibid., pp. 38-41). Jesus' experience is the archetype of the experience of Latin American Christians whose powerlessness in the face of totalitarian regimes results in the martyrdom of the "disappeared."

[77]Boff, *Passion*, p. 45.   [78]Ibid., p. 52.   [79]Ibid., p. 65.   [80]Ibid., pp. 70-85.

[81]Ibid., pp. 100-01.   [82]Ibid., p. 102.   [83]Ibid., p. 115. See appendix.

[84]Ibid., p. 122.   [85]Boff, *Liberator*, p. 118.   [86]Boff, *Passion*, p. 66.

[87]Ibid.   [88]Boff, *Liberator*, p. 122.   [89]Ibid., p. 129.   [90]Boff, *Passion*, p. 67.

[91]Ibid., pp. 66-67.

[92]Cf. Pannenberg, *Jesus*, p. 247: "Thus, the meaning of his death could only be understood as an expression of service to humanity in the name of the love of God revealed in his message, which determined his whole mission."

[93]Boff, *Liberator*, p. 133.   [94]Ibid.

[95]Quoted in Boff, *Evangelho*, p. 37. Portuguese original: ". . . eixo central de convergência universal e ponto preciso de encontro que surge entre o universo e o ponto Omêga" (trans. Martha J. Spiegel).

[96]Boff, *Liberator*, p. 135.

[97]Ibid., pp. 134-35. Cf. Boff, *Passion*, p. 67: "The resurrection is not only the event that glorifies and justifies Jesus Christ, his truth, and his attitudes. It is also the manifestation of what the reign of God is in its plenitude: the epiphany of the future that God has promised. It is the demonstration of what men and women can hope for, because it is God who has promised it to them."

[98]Boff, *Ressurreição*, p. 105. Portuguese original: "Agora pela ressurreição o homem é desobstaculizado e irrompe (se para a vida eterna) a perfeita e cabal adequação espirito-corpo-mundo, sem as limitações espacio-temporais e as alienações da história do pecado" (trans. Martha J. Spiegel).

[99]Ibid., p. 104.   [100]Boff, *Liberator*, p. 137.   [101]Boff, *Liberating Grace*.

[102]Boff, *Passion*, p. 68.

[103]Leonardo Boff, *The Question of Faith in the Resurrection of Jesus*, trans. Luis Runde (Chicago, Ill: Franciscan Herald Press, 1971), p. 36.

[104]Ibid., pp. 37-38.   [105]Boff, *Liberator*, pp. 142-44.

[106]Ibid., p. 147.   [107]Ibid., p. 150.   [108]Ibid., p. 155.   [109]Ibid., p. 149.

[110]Ibid., p. 162.   [111]Ibid., p. 163.

[112]See ibid., pp. 163-73, for Boff's "demythologization" of the infancy narratives.

[113]Boff, *Passion*, p. 68.   [114]Ibid.   [115]Boff, *Liberator*, pp. 176-77.

[116]Ibid., p. 177.   [117]Ibid., p. 182.   [118]Ibid., p. 180.   [119]Ibid., p. 194.

[120]Ibid., pp. 183-88.   [121]Ibid., p. 189-90.   [122]Ibid., p. 191.   [123]Ibid.

[124]Ibid., pp. 191-92.   [125]Ibid., pp. 192-94.

[126]At this point Boff seems to contradict himself. He has gone to great lengths to point out the full humanity of Jesus which would include, in the Council's terminology, a hypostasis "enduring in himself and for himself" (ibid., p. 196). To this writer, Boff's point is not the absence of a hypostasis *per se*, but of an egotistical one that would cause Jesus to turn in upon himself and away from others.

[127]Boff, *Liberator*, p. 197.   [128]Ibid.

[129]Piet Schoonenberg, *The Christ: A Study of the God-Man Relationship in the Whole of Creation and in Jesus Christ*, trans. Della Couling (New York: Herder and Herder, 1971), p. 66.

[130]Ibid., p. 87.

[131]Boff, *Liberator*, p. 199. This reversal parallels Boff's contention that the birth narratives were written last and constituted the end of the primitive community's re-examination of Jesus' life in light of the resurrection.

132Boff, *Liberator*, pp. 204-05.   133Ibid., pp. 199-200.   134Ibid., p. 201.

135Ibid., p. 202. One must be aware of the line Boff's reasoning takes. He does not say that Jesus did not sin because he could not sin. That would be starting with the incarnation and following the logic of an *a priori* understanding of the word, "God." Instead, Boff begins with the life of Jesus, culminating in the crucifixion and resurrection, and concludes that Jesus did not sin. It was Jesus' "intimate and uninterrupted union with God," his continual openness to God, that kept him from sinning. In light of this, Boff says that Jesus could not sin only because he, in fact, did not sin.

136Boff, *Liberator*, p. 202.   137Ibid., p. 203.   138Ibid., p. 204.   139Ibid., p. 207.

140Ibid.

141See Boff, *Evangelho*, pp. 71-78, for a fuller discussion of this type of Christology.

142Boff, *Liberator*, p. 212.

143Ibid., p. 216. While this type of thinking may seem superfluous, it does broaden the scope of theology by pointing out that there is more mystery than knowledge vis-à-vis the cosmos.

144Boff, *Liberator*, p. 218. Boff is indebted to Karl Rahner's discussion of "anonymous Christians" and "implicit Christianity" at this point. See Karl Rahner, "Anonymous Christians," *Thelogical Investigations*, Vol. VI, trans. Karl-H. and Boniface Kruger (Baltimore: Helicon Press, 1969), pp. 390-98 and Karl Rahner, "Atheism and Implicit Christianity," *Theological Investigations*, Vol. IX, trans. Graham Harrison (London: Darton, Longman and Todd, 1972), pp. 145-64.

145Boff, *Liberator*, p. 212.   146Ibid.   147Ibid., p. 219.   148Ibid.

149Ibid., p. 257.   150Ibid., p. 220.   151Ibid., pp. 220-21.

152Ibid., p. 257.   153Ibid., p. 222.   154Ibid.

155Ibid., pp. 257-58. This impacts the christological process today in two ways. First, it broadens the horizons in which Christ is at work: in the cosmos, other religions, and in local church situations. Second, new situations require new insights and new ways of describing reality. Since the cosmic Christ is at work in all people and in all areas of life, all of life is sacralized. Areas of life once thought to be separate from theology now provide theological data.

156Boff, *Liberator*, pp. 234-45.

157Boff, *Evangelho*, p. 79. Portuguese original: "Disso tudo se segue que a criação tem, em seu ser mais íntimo, traços críticos, espelha em miríades de facêtas diferentes o mesmo rosto e forma como que o corpo cósmico de Cristo" (trans. Martha J. Spiegel).

158Leonardo Boff, *Ecclesiogenesis: The Base Communities Reinvent the Church*, trans. Robert R. Barr (Maryknoll: Orbis Books, 1986). Cited hereafter as *Ecclesiogenesis*.

159Leonardo Boff, *Church: Charism and Power: Liberation Theology and the Institutional Church*, trans. John W. Diercksmeier (New York: Crossroad, 1986). Cited hereafter as *Church*.

160Boff, *Ecclesiogenesis*, p. 2.   161Ibid., p. 4.   162Boff, *Church*, p. 9.

163Boff, *Ecclesiogenesis*, p. 11.   164Boff, *Church*, p. 124.

165Leonardo Boff, *Way of the Cross--Way of Justice*, trans. John Drury (Maryknoll: Orbis Books, 1980). If, as Boff contends, the stations of the cross apply to the Christian life, then a careful weighing of the costs is necessary before beginning discipleship. To call for love, justice, mercy, and humble service to God will provoke the powers that be (religious, political, social, or economic) to insure, by any means necessary, their privileged position.

166Boff, *Ecclesiogenesis*, p. 7.   167Ibid., p. 15.   168Ibid., p. 26.

169Boff, *Church*, p. 159.   170Ibid.   171Boff, *Ecclesiogenesis*, p. 25.

172Boff, *Church*, pp. 101-02.

173Boff, *Liberating Grace*, p. 40: Boff defined grace as *scientia* (knowledge) and *conscientia* (awareness). In other words, grace was knowledge of events coordinated into a systematic world view.

174Ibid., p. 4.   175Ibid., pp. 8-9.   176Ibid., p. 184.

177This is not to say that theological reflection upon the experience of grace should not occur. Boff devotes over half of his book to just such an endeavor. His point is that the purpose of this reflection is to facilitate the *experience* of grace and not just talk *about* grace.

178Boff, *Liberating Grace*, p. 60.   179Ibid., p. 28.

180Boff, *Liberating Grace*, pp. 90-104. For example, chance, creativity, imagination, success, and festivals. See also Leonardo Boff, *Sacraments of Life, Life of the Sacraments*, trans. John Drury (Washington, D. C.: The Pastoral Press, 1987) where Boff sacramentally interprets such things as "our family mug," "my father's cigarette butt," and "a schoolteacher."

Chapter 3

JESUS CHRIST, THE WAY OF THE SON:
THE CHRISTOLOGY OF JON SOBRINO

This chapter is concerned with the Christology of Jon Sobrino. It begins with a brief biographical sketch of Sobrino's life, followed by a critical analysis of his Christology. The chapter ends with a discussion of the impact of Sobrino's Christology on his theology.

Biographical Sketch

Jon Sobrino was born in 1938, in Barcelona, Spain, to a Basque family during the Spanish Civil War. In 1956 he was ordained a Jesuit priest and emigrated to El Salvador. He received his master's degree in Engineering Mechanics from St. Louis University in 1965. Sobrino earned his doctorate in theology from the Hochschule Sankt Georgen in Frankfurt in 1975. His thesis was entitled *Le Dieu Crucifie*.

Sobrino is now professor of philosophy and theology at the Universidad José Simeón Cañas in San Salvador, El Salvador. He is the director of the Center for Theological Reflection and contributes regularly to the journals *Estudio Centroamericanos* and *Christus*.[1] He is the author of several books, including *Christology at the Crossroads*, *Jesus in Latin America*, and *The True Church and the Poor*.

Methodology

Sobrino's concern for methodology is rooted in his perception of a "crisis of existence" in the Latin American Church. This crisis goes to the very root of Christian existence: Jesus Christ and the God who is revealed in him. Thus, the basic question Christology must answer is Jesus' own, "Who do you say that I am?" Sobrino's answer to this question is drawn from the New Testament, tradition, especially conciliar dogmatic statements, new historical contexts, and the manifestation of the Spirit in "the signs of the times."[2] To implement this methodology, Sobrino contends that Christology must be "ecclesial, historical, and trinitarian."

Ecclesial Christology follows the example of the New Testament. It includes both:

the way Christ is conceived on the basis of the concrete life and reality of a given community, and . . . the meaning of a given community's life and activity as seen from the standpoint of Christ.[3]

Thus, Sobrino's Christology reflects the life and praxis of the base communities of Latin America. He does not ignore the christological dogmas of the Church; but they are a "second stage" in an ecclesial Christology. Their purpose is to guarantee "truth *about* Christ." But if Christians, individually and communally, "are to have *real first-hand knowledge of Christ* . . . as formulated in dogma . . . then they simply must reconsider Christ from the standpoint of their own situation and activity."[4]

A historical Christology has three aspects. First, its "logical procedure" is chronological. It begins with the historical Jesus and re-traces the steps the church took to arrive at its confession that "Jesus is Lord." The second aspect is the use of "historical categories," specifically "sin and conflict," in order to understand Jesus. This presupposes a "process of evolution" within Jesus in both his human development and in his relationship with God. The final aspect is "the relational nature of Jesus." His primary focal point was the kingdom of God and its realization. Therefore, a historical Christology must include the past, present, and future, and their relationship to God's coming kingdom.[5]

Finally, Sobrino contends that "*we cannot do Christology at all except within the framework of the trinitarian reality of God.*"[6] Christology is "theological" in that God and God's kingdom are the ultimate reference points for Jesus and, therefore, the "ultimate horizon" of human history. Christology is "christological" in that "strictly speaking . . . . [Jesus] is the revelation of the Son, of the proper way to approach and correspond to the Father."[7] Christology is "pneumatological" in that Jesus and God are known only by living life in accordance with the Spirit of Jesus. Without this trinitarian foundation, Jesus' praxis is incomprehensible, the work of the Spirit is vague, and God becomes "abstract and manipulable."[8]

The Starting Point: The Historical Jesus

Sobrino's Christology begins with the historical Jesus, which raises the problem of hermeneutics. This is an important issue because:

the problem of choosing a starting point becomes the quest for some focus on Christ that will best reveal him in his universality and do so in concrete rather than abstract terms.[9]

As this chapter will show, the concreteness of the starting point is crucial, not its universality. In other words, Sobrino utilizes an inductive approach in his Christology. Once he establishes the specificity of the starting point, he can proceed to Christ's universal appeal.

Sobrino critically examines seven possible starting points for constructing

Christology. They are: 1) the dogmatic formulations of Chalcedon; 2) a more biblical focus upon Christ's titles or his major life events; 3) the experience of Christ in cultic worship; 4) the resurrection as the culmination of Christ's earthly life; 5) the kerygmatic Christ; 6) Jesus' teachings; and 7) soteriology.[10] While acknowledging the value of these methodologies for Christology, Sobrino still rejects them as starting points. The reason is that they all point to a common antecedent: the historical Jesus.[11]

For Sobrino, the historical Jesus is found in his "person, teaching, attitudes, and deeds . . . insofar as they are accessible, in a more or less general way, to historical and exegetical investigation."[12] Sobrino makes this choice for several reasons. First, it avoids abstractions and their possible manipulations of the Christ event. Second, church history has shown that the essence of Christian faith is in danger when the historical Jesus is neglected for the Christ of faith. Third, the historical Jesus is the hermeneutic principle uniting knowledge of Christ and real-life praxis. Fourth, there is a "noticeable resemblance" between the time of Jesus and modern-day Latin America. Finally, New Testament Christologies themselves are elliptical; they revolve around the foci of Jesus of Nazareth and the concrete situation of each community.[13]

Sobrino's decision to begin with the historical Jesus raises several exegetical issues. New Testament scholarship has shown that the authors of the Gospels wove together different traditions, world views, and communal situations in their presentations of Jesus. How, then, can Sobrino claim to know the "historical" Jesus?

Sobrino recognizes that the Gospels are the products of faith. He also realizes that the history of theology has shown the difficulty of finding "the historical-Jesus-in-himself." He contends, however, that Latin American Christology is not searching for the *ipsissima verba* or *ipsissima facta* of Jesus of Nazareth. The intent of liberation Christology:

> consists in discovering and historically insuring the basic structure of his practice . . . an end through which the basic structure of his internal historicity and his person are likewise discernible.[14]

This intent reflects a dialectic that liberation Christology finds in the New Testament itself. On the one hand, Jesus of Nazareth "cannot be theologized without being historicized"; which is to say, Jesus cannot be confessed as the Christ without reference to his earthly life. On the other hand, Jesus "cannot be historicized without being theologized"; which is to say, the events of Jesus' life lead to the confession that he is the Christ.[15]

Sobrino is indebted to Edward Schillebeeckx for the criteria he uses to discover and historically insure the praxis of Jesus. "The appearance of one and the same theme on various levels of tradition" is the first criterion. The meaning of this point is self-evident. The second criterion, "what is specific to and distinctive of a theme by contrast with and even in opposition to theologies and practices that come after Jesus" is not so obvious. In other words, reflection upon Jesus' words and deeds, even in a hostile or negative environment, actually serves to keep attention focused upon his praxis. "The consistency of Jesus' death with what is narrated of his life" is the final criterion and it is especially relevant to Latin American Christians. Thousands of Latin Americans have died attempting to follow Jesus' praxis. Therefore, he must have lived a life like the one presented in the Gospels.16

On the basis of the intent of Latin American Christology and the above criteria, the following aspects of Jesus' life are accepted as historical by Sobrino:

> on the level of event, Jesus' baptism by John, a certain initial success in his ministry, some early conflicts, the selection and dispatch of a group of followers, the use of parables, a crisis toward the middle or end of his public life, the journey to Jerusalem, some kind of meal with those close to him, his arrest, and his crucifixion, with words written on a placard attached to the cross; on the level of behavior, certain attitudes toward the Jewish Law and the Temple, toward the marginalized, the possessed, those in power, certain practices of healing and approach to sinners, the demand for conversion and discipleship, certain specific attitudes toward the kingdom of God and the God of the kingdom; on the level of word, key words and phrases like Abba, "kingdom of God," "follow me," and so on.17

Stated in this way, Sobrino's picture of the historical Jesus does not differ significantly from other views found in contemporary Christology. He differs, however, in the way he interprets Jesus' life and its significance for those who would follow him.

Hermeneutical Guideposts
    for Christology

This different interpretation of the historical Jesus is based upon the hermeneutic Sobrino employs, which has five points or guideposts. The first is *"the theological milieu of the author."* How does one view theology and its relationship to the other aspects of one's culture? The second guidepost is the author's *"attitude toward . . . the Enlightenment."* Did this event promote the "autonomy of reason" over all external authorities? Or did it espouse the "autonomy of the whole person" over alienating structures? *"The kind of hermeneutics used by an author"* is the next guidepost. Is it existential, transcendental, or revolutionary? Does it include both the truth or falsity of historical affirmations and the understanding and interpretation of them, or just the former? The fourth guidepost is *"the way in which the fundamental metaphysical quandary is posed."* Is it a question of natural theology or a question of theodicy? The final guidepost is *"the density of an author's christological concentration."* Is Christology central to the understanding of the basic concepts of theology or is it one among many?18

The issue now is to see how these guideposts shape Latin American Christology. The theological milieu of the Latin American theologian is comprised of the intersection of life and faith. More specifically, how does faith relate to the facts of oppression and underdevelopment? This situation leads directly to an understanding of the Enlightenment in terms of its second stage, that of espousing the autonomy of the person vis-à-vis alienating structures. The hermeneutic employed in liberation Christology is informed by praxis, praxis defined as "actions . . . designed to operate on [one's] surrounding historical circumstances in order to change them in a specific direction."[19] Specifically Christian praxis results from the study of Jesus' intentions combined with traditional exegetical study to arrive at an "effective collaboration" with Jesus' own praxis. The fundamental metaphysical quandary is summarized by the word "liberation." Liberation, however, is more than a new slant on theodicy. It denotes a striving after God's kingdom in order to eradicate oppression. At the time of Sobrino's *Christologia desde america latina* (1976), the christological concentration of liberation theology was hotly debated. It is beyond the scope of this book to enumerate the reasons for this debate, Sobrino contends that Christology is the center of liberation theology. All that has been written concerning "the Latin American situation" was based upon the proclamation and praxis of the historical Jesus.[20]

Jesus of Nazareth

This section deals with issues that concern the historical Jesus. Familiar themes, such as the kingdom of God, Jesus' death, and resurrection, will be analyzed. New themes, such as Jesus' faith and prayer will, also be introduced and examined.

The Kingdom of God

Sobrino agrees with modern New Testament scholarship that Jesus' own preaching focused on the kingdom of God. On the one hand, Jesus did not preach about himself. On the other hand, he did not simply talk about God: he talked about the kingdom of God. This is another example of the concept of relationality in Sobrino's Christology. He argues that historically:

> we can only come to know the historical Jesus in and through the notion of God's kingdom. By the same token we can only come to understand what is meant by the kingdom of God through Jesus.[21]

Sobrino's intention is to avoid *a priori* understandings of God's kingdom and of Jesus' proclamation of the kingdom.

This view of the relationship between Jesus and God's kingdom has several results. Jesus' deeds are seen as liberating; the "original unity" of the vertical and horizontal aspects of Christian faith is clear. This position makes following Jesus, understood as praxis, the hermeneutic principle for understanding who God is and who the Christ of faith is. This hermeneutic allows Jesus to define "divinity" rather than vice versa. This view sees Jesus the Son as "the way to the Father." But Jesus as "the way" is accessible only insofar as one is willing to follow his course.[22]

Sobrino discusses the nature of God's kingdom in relation to history, grace, sin, and conversion.[23] Throughout this discussion, he offers no definition of the kingdom, something Jesus did not do either. For Jesus, the kingdom is good news for the poor and is composed of the poor. As such, the kingdom is a message of hope and love. It offers the hope that the present situation of deprivation is not God's last word to the poor. It is love because God has set them apart to receive the kingdom first.[24] Methodologically, then, "the poor, sinners, and the despised are the necessary, though not absolutely sufficient, starting point for an understanding of what is meant by the good news of the kingdom."[25] God's partiality toward the poor is what guarantees the church's message that God loves humankind and that Jesus is the savior of all.[26] If God can take care of the "least of these," God is capable of caring for all.

On the surface this description of the kingdom of God appears to be ahistorical, a view which Sobrino wishes to avoid at all costs; but the term itself evokes an intimate relationship with history. Israel recognized God's lordship over history because of God's liberating acts toward Israel. Thus, "kingdom of God" has two key connotations: 1) God rules history through dynamic acts; and 2) the purpose of God's rule is to modify the present order of things and to establish a determinate order.[27] This dynamic element becomes more important when viewed in light of Israel's history from the destruction of the two kingdoms up to Jesus' day. This history caused a crisis of faith because it was incompatible with Israel's experience of God. It gave rise to the eschatological hope for a change in Israel's situation. Israel began to look for the Messiah and authentic liberation.[28]

Apocalypticism also played a role in the development of Israel's perception of the kingdom. Not only did it evoke hope for a new creation, it also signaled the end of history. Even though the kingdom was hidden, "human beings can calculate when it will manifest itself and even hasten its coming, even though it remains the exclusive work of God."[29]

Thus, political history and apocalyptic hope form the context of Jesus' presentation of the definitive reign of God. This reign is near at hand and is already dawning: it is an extension of human potentialities; it is grace; it is a transformation of the inner person; it is a restructuring of all human relationships; it is authentic liberation on every level of existence. In all of this, God is acting, revealing Godself in concrete historical situations. Sobrino concludes from this that God's actions reflect God's being. The purpose of God's liberative acts toward humanity is to establish reconciliation between human beings; the divine-human relationship has a direct impact upon human relationships.[30]

This idea of action's reflecting being is the linch pin that unites Jesus' words and deeds. Since God's reign includes God's acting, words alone cannot proclaim God's kingdom. Orthopraxis is necessary. Sobrino contends that this relationship between word and deed stems from Jesus' experience of God as "Abba." For Sobrino, God cannot be "Abba" if a community of brothers and sisters is not created.[31] In other words, God's kingdom is not dawning if a healing of human relationships does not occur. That would be proof that God is not acting.

The second aspect Sobrino notes concerning the kingdom is its graciousness. He contends that Jesus differed from his contemporaries (John the

Baptist, Pharisees, Zealots, and Essenes) by proclaiming the kingdom as good news and grace. The kingdom is grace in two ways. First, the coming of the kingdom is due to God's initiative. Following the Law, evicting the Romans, or heeding "the signs of the times" cannot establish the kingdom--that is God's work. Second, the salvation and liberation wrought by the kingdom must be expressed in deeds as well as in words. As Sobrino says, "God is insofar as he acts, insofar as he alters reality; and we must view the *actions* of Jesus in that light. . . . They are meant to demonstrate the kingdom of God."[32] As such, the kingdom of God is the primary determinant of what Jesus does.

Therefore, the actions of Jesus are signs of the coming of the kingdom in grace. In response to John the Baptist's question concerning his messiahship, Jesus' answer "presupposes that the kingdom is the transformation . . . of an oppressive situation, and that God's activity can only be envisioned as the *overcoming* of a negative situation."[33] This explains why the Gospels place Jesus in conflictive situations: to show the discontinuity between the way things are and the good news of the kingdom's liberation. So Jesus goes to the sick, the despised, foreigners, women, and the demon possessed. They help him reveal the total transforming power of the coming kingdom.[34]

Once again Sobrino has employed the concept of relationality. The nature of the kingdom allows Jesus' miracles and forgiveness of sins to identify indirectly who he is. According to Sobrino, both types of actions "*are primarily signs of the arrival of the kingdom of God. They are signs of liberation, and only in that context can they help to shed light on the person of Jesus.*"[35] This is why the Gospels describe Jesus' miracles as *dynamis, ergon,* and *semeion*: "they are preaching about the kingdom in deeds, in which the nearness of God is made concrete and visible."[36] The same holds true for Jesus' forgiveness of sins. Forgiveness is usually extended to one in need, someone "living under oppression, the person . . . despised by those who are just in society according to the law and who is condemned to a life with no future by the law itself."[37]

The relationship of the kingdom of God to sin is the third aspect of Jesus' proclamation that Sobrino examines. Theologically, sin is the rejection of God's coming reign, which is rejected because it comes as a future one cannot control. Anthropologically, sin is the exercise of one's power to secure oneself against God by oppressing others; therefore, sin has two dimensions: the personal and the social. The former is a refusal to accept God's future, while the latter is a refusal to anticipate that future within history. The anathemas pronounced by Jesus against the religious and political rulers of his day reflect these two dimensions. His judgments are not aimed at individuals. Rather, they are directed against group manifestations of an egotism contrary to the kingdom of grace, against the use of power to maintain the status quo.[38]

Hence, for Jesus, the essence of sin is the egocentric will to power. If Sobrino is correct in saying that God's power is seen in liberative actions that create a community of brothers and sisters, then any power not dedicated to the service and well-being of others is sin. The assertion of one's power over others is simply the outward manifestation of a previous, internal, assertion of one's works against God's gracious kingdom.[39] In other words, it is impossible to love God, who is unseen, if one does not love (as oneself) the person one can see.

The final observation Sobrino makes concerning Jesus' proclamation of the kingdom deals with conversion. The issue at stake is how to balance the dialectic between the kingdom's being the exclusive work of God and human "*metanoia*." Sobrino finds the balance in two complementary attitudes toward conversion. The first attitude was embodied by the "poor" or "lowly." These people are the ones whose lives are exploited by others, offering them no hope for the future. They were called simply to have faith, to hope in the future because there were possibilities still open to God. For Sobrino, this fundamental call to faith applies to everyone because everyone endures some form of oppression. Therefore, faith is not an arbitrary demand made by Jesus.[40] Rather, it is "the element of utopian hope that renders present as totally 'other' the God who is not merely in continuity with our potentialities."[41]

The second attitude was embodied by the people who heard in Jesus' preaching a call to discipleship: not only must they have faith, they must also be actively involved in proclaiming and actualizing God's kingdom. This call had two stages. In the first, the Twelve, the eschatological Israel, was sent out with power to work signs attesting to the presence of the kingdom. This is in keeping with a Jewish orthodoxy that anticipated a restoration of the Davidic monarchy by the Messiah. But the growing conflict between Jesus and the scribes and Pharisees caused an epistemological break with that orthodoxy by both Jesus and his disciples. The work of implanting the kingdom began to assume the form of work associated with the Suffering Servant of Yahweh. Even though Jesus is separate from the kingdom insofar as he is its proclaimer and the catalyst for discipleship, now he is the criterion for discipleship.[42] As Sobrino says, "Now [Jesus] is also the new, unknown, and painful way--the only way--in which one can come to understand that God is drawing near to human beings and how he is doing it."[43]

This attitude has two concrete implications. The first implication is based on Sobrino's idea that God's actions reveal God's being. If the God of Jesus is actively involved in the liberation and reconciliation of human beings, then "access to God" is possible only if one's praxis is based upon following Jesus' own praxis. The second implication follows closely upon the first. God, the kingdom of God, and Jesus' own person cannot be known solely through orthodoxy; knowledge must be coupled with action.[44]

"The Faith of Jesus"

Jesus' own faith is not usually a part of Christology, probably due to the influence of a Christology "from above." The Christ-event begins with the Incarnation, with God's becoming human. Jesus' words and deeds are a call to repent and accept God's salvation. Jesus himself does not exhibit faith in God because he is the object of faith. Thus, the emphasis is upon Jesus' divinity rather than his humanity.

But Sobrino's choice to begin his Christology with the historical Jesus means starting with Jesus' humanity. Even so, "humanity" is still too general.

Sobrino wants Jesus' humanity to be as particular as possible. To accomplish this, Sobrino posits three guidelines to aid in interpreting and understanding the faith of Jesus:

> 1. Every human action in history . . . is guided by certain values as basically good at the start. . . . Hence the historical course of a person must entail the concretion of those values which triggered that course.

> 2. Change and conflict are part of every movement in history. Historical concretion, then, is a dialectical process carried out in the presence of opposing, negative factors that must be overcome. . . .

> 3. In the historical process we find a dialectical interplay between fashioning reality and fashioning oneself as an active subject.[45]

In other words, Sobrino intends to paint a picture of Jesus' faith based upon the embodiment of his relationship to the kingdom of God and to the God of the kingdom.

To be sure, these points are self-evident in a general way; everyone wrestles with individuation in the maturation process. Sobrino's concern is to concretize them vis-à-vis the Latin American dialectic of faith and oppression. First, the issue in Latin America is the problem of moving from an inherited faith to a new concrete faith that is truly liberative. Second, the conflict-ridden nature of Jesus' faith is mirrored in the experience of Latin American Christians vis-à-vis existing power structures. Finally, faith is a dialectic between actively participating in actualizing the kingdom and passively being defined by it.[46]

Sobrino divides "the history of Jesus' faith" into two stages, before and after the so-called Galilean crisis. In the first stage, Jesus did not differ significantly from other rabbis. His teachings are grounded in Jewish orthodoxy. He does not go against the Law and the prophets. He does, however, bring a new slant to them via his relationship to God's kingdom. The kingdom represents the possibility of human "filiation with the Father." Therefore, Jesus advocates doing deeds that effect human reconciliation, which is the ultimate goal of the kingdom.[47]

The transition between the two stages occurs in several interdependent ways. The religious leaders do not accept Jesus or his message. The people reject his radicalization of the kingdom as *the* reference point for living a life faithful to God. These two rejections reveal that God and God's kingdom are not getting any closer. Jesus has failed in his mission as he first conceived it.[48]

The second stage begins when Jesus leaves Galilee for Caesarea Philippi and the towns of the Decapolis. This geographical break is the outward expression of an internal re-evaluation of his faith and mission. Jesus now begins to talk about his death. He begins to concentrate upon his disciples. Discipleship is re-defined in terms of self-sacrifice.[49]

Thus, the second stage is not merely a continuation of the first. God's kingdom remains Jesus' historical reference point; but he no longer sees the kingdom as imminent. Serving the kingdom means placing his life on the line, even to the point of accepting his death as part of that service. The power he now wields is the power of love in suffering. The God of the kingdom remains as a reference point, also. But Jesus' faith in God become a "trust against trust"; he cannot base his trust upon historical circumstances. Faithfulness to God's mission is viewed in light of the possibility of Jesus' imminent death rather than the imminent establishment of God's kingdom. Jesus' attitude toward sin also changes in light of the different relationships he now has with God and the kingdom. Instead of prophetic denunciation, Jesus must bear the burden of sin itself; he must feel its power and be led to the cross. Discipleship is not only the proclamation of the kingdom by words and deeds; it is also an invitation to take up one's cross as did Jesus. In other words, the elements of Jesus' faith, God, the kingdom of God, and discipleship remain the same in both stages. What has changed is Jesus' relationship to, and understanding of, those elements.50

Faith, then, is a process, an "ongoing search" for God and God's kingdom. Since this process is historical, it entails temptation and ignorance. These two possibilities form what Sobrino calls "the human condition of Jesus' faith," for this is the environment in which human beings live. For Jesus, temptation was a constant companion. He was faced continually with the option of defining his person by surrendering to God or by rejecting God; to live for himself or to live for others. The Gospel writers telescoped this aspect of Jesus' life into his wilderness temptations. Their placement is important because they follow immediately upon his awareness of his mission and sonship.51

The use of power is the direct issue of the temptations. Will Jesus be a false messiah and use his power to force the kingdom upon people? Or will he be the true messiah and use his power to free people from their many oppressions in favor of the kingdom? Indirectly, Jesus' temptations reveal his conception of the true nature of God. God does not control history and humanity from the outside; rather, God works within the bounds of history, giving Godself in self-surrender to humanity.52

Up to this point, Sobrino's treatment of Jesus' temptations is fairly traditional: Jesus was constantly confronted with the issue of how to embody God's kingdom. The difference arises in his contention that the dialogue in these temptations is actually between Jesus and God. Satan is only the medium by which this conversation occurs. One reason for this assertion is that Satan knows Jesus and the nature of his mission. It is Jesus who must wrestle with the insights gained at his baptism. Therefore, the temptations are theological in nature for they are concerned with Jesus' relationship to God. Another reason is that the Old Testament references in the temptations clearly point out that the issue is "Jesus' conception of God and God's kingdom." Functionally speaking, these temptations force Jesus to decide how he will concretely carry out his mission.53

Jesus' bouts with temptation becomes critical in Gethsemane and in his ensuing passion. Conflicts with religious and political power structures have become more intense and the disciples are armed. It seems that only force (egocentric use of power) can save him and his cause. His conception of God's kingdom is also in crisis. Service to the kingdom has shifted from overcoming

Satan to succumbing to sin's power. Consequently, Jesus' view of God is in flux, also. His gracious God has abandoned him and demands his life.[54] Jesus overcomes the temptation of idolatry by accepting the fact that faith means "total self surrender and that liberative love should mean a love fraught with suffering."[55]

Sobrino's treatment of Jesus' temptations only adds to their traditional understanding. The same cannot be said for his discussion of ignorance, the second human condition of Jesus' faith. At this point Sobrino radically concretizes Jesus' humanity and his solidarity with humanity. He does so by questioning the Greek idea that ignorance is an imperfection of being. Sobrino argues that ignorance as an "*anthropological* dimension" in Jesus does not present too great an obstacle. He bases this conclusion on Luke 2:52. Growth and maturation involve learning, which implies that one lacks knowledge. Therefore, Jesus had to learn to speak, to walk, to work, to relate to others, and so on. In light of this, ignorance is not opposed to the perfection, or maturation, of one's being--not even for Jesus![56]

Ignorance becomes an issue when its theological import is examined. The Gospels portray Jesus ignorant vis-à-vis "the core of his own person and his mission," that is, the kingdom of God.[57] He does not know when it will arrive, but says some of his followers will see it. From a Greek perspective this is "the height of imperfection." How could Jesus, God incarnate, be mistaken about the timing of God's kingdom? Sobrino contends that this is not a problem for biblical faith; in fact, it is the essence of faith because it lets God be God. By trusting in God, in spite of his ignorance concerning the kingdom, Jesus reveals his true humanity and his sonship as the firstborn of faith.[58]

The significance of Jesus' faith for Christology is evident in three ways. First, the faith of Jesus reformulates the concept of his divinity. For Sobrino, Jesus' divinity derives from his "*relationship* to the Father" rather than to the Logos. The relational character of Jesus' divinity entails a dynamic conception of "divine nature" because it is dependent upon Jesus' fidelity to his mission to proclaim and actualize God's kingdom. Second, Jesus' faith means that he is the revelation of the Son of God and of the way one becomes a child of God; thus, Jesus is the "firstborn" of faith. Sobrino revives this concept because it signifies Jesus' relationship to both God and humanity; Jesus is both "Son" and "brother." If "brotherliness" is not a part of Jesus' divinity, then Jesus is not the Son. Third, the faith of Jesus makes the difference between Jesus and his sisters and brothers historical rather than ontological. Jesus lived "faith in all its pristine fullness" in a concrete historical life, thereby opening the "pathway of faith" for others to traverse.[59]

"The Prayer of Jesus"

Another aspect of Sobrino's Christology that differs from traditional ones is his discussion of "the prayer of Jesus." Sobrino does not reveal anything new about prayer itself. Its significance lies in his contention that this is the way Jesus himself prayed, and not just what he taught about prayer. Sobrino proceeds along two lines. First, he uses Jesus' criticism of certain prayers to deduce three characteristics of true prayer. He then examines two of Jesus' own prayers.

The first characteristic of true prayer is that it is other-oriented. The focus of prayer is upon God and other people; the self is not the subject or object of prayer. The second characteristic is "theological poverty before God," that is, humility; prayer is not merely words directed to God. The practice of justice is the converse of prayer's verbal side. Finally, true prayer is a seeking after God's will; it is neither an attempt to manipulate God into acting a certain way nor an excuse for unjust activities.[60]

Turning to Jesus' own prayer, Sobrino notes two different patterns in the Synoptics. The first merely states that Jesus prayed. Sobrino takes this to mean two things. First, Jesus prayed as would any pious Israelite: at meals, Sabbath worship, and other proscribed times. Second, Jesus prayed at times of important decisions: his baptism, choosing the Twelve, teaching the "Our Father," on occasion of his miracles, and in Gethsemane.[61]

The second pattern is composed of the prayers Jesus himself prayed. Sobrino focuses on two of those prayers. The first, a prayer of praise and thanksgiving, is found in Matthew 11:25 and Luke 10:21. In this prayer, Jesus offers praise to God for the understanding that is found in the least likely place, among the poor. Sobrino contends that this prayer can be fully understood only against the backdrop of the apocalypticism of the book of Daniel. In Daniel 2, there is thanksgiving for the communication of a revelation concerning the kingdom of God. In light of this, Jesus is thankful that his proclamation of God's kingdom to the poor has been understood and accepted by them. An element of scandal resides in this realization because it reveals God's partiality to the oppressed. This scandalous element "cannot be neglected or avoided if one wants to gain access to the Father of Jesus specifically rather than to some deity in the abstract."[62]

The second prayer Sobrino examines is Jesus' prayer in Gethsemane. Jesus is undergoing a crisis of meaning: has he truly understood God and God's kingdom? He is not merely wrestling with the possibility of his own death, but with death as the consequence of his life. Must his proclamation of good news to the poor, his prophetic denunciation of unjust power structures, and his perception of God's drawing near in grace call for his death? Jesus' answer to these questions was fidelity to his mission. Sobrino puts it this way:

> His trust in the Father would remain alive in the very depths of his passion even though he did not want the Father's will to take the form of the cross, and even though he did not know for sure who this Father was that would demand his death and later abandon him on the cross.[63]

For Sobrino, the reason for this choice lay in Jesus' ignorance: he had to trust in God the same way any other human being would.[64]

One aspect of Sobrino's discussion of Jesus' prayer is troublesome: namely, he does not include "the Lord's prayer." Clark Williamson asks: "What prayer could be more authentic from the criterion of liberating praxis?"[65] If any of Jesus' prayers would fit the characteristics of true prayer, it would be this one. Not only that, but it would also coalesce with Sobrino's emphasis upon the kingdom of God as the primary pole of reference for Jesus' praxis. There can be no doubt that

Sobrino's discussion of Jesus' prayers would have been enriched by its inclusion.

The question of the identity of the God of Jesus' prayer arises at this point. Sobrino's view of God will be discussed near the end of this chapter, however, it is necessary to say something on that subject now. According to Sobrino, Jesus' God is a transcendent God whose essence is love.[66] Transcendence is indirectly revealed by the fact that Jesus relates to God as the God of the kingdom, which is not of this world. In its fullness and in its partial embodiments, its purpose is to transform the world in accordance with God's will. Thus, Jesus' God cannot be known in abstraction, but only by God's liberative acts in history. That God's essence is love is indirectly revealed by the fact that God's kingdom is drawing near in grace. As Sobrino pointed out, Jesus proclaimed the kingdom as good news rather than judgment. In his words he called for faith in a God who is not bound by historical circumstances. In his deeds he revealed that God is concerned with both the spiritual and physical well-being of people.[67]

The Self-Consciousness
of Jesus

An analysis of Sobrino's view of the self-consciousness of Jesus is now appropriate. He approaches this subject indirectly: that is, by way of Jesus' relationship to the kingdom of God and of his relationship to God. An important part of his understanding of Jesus' self-consciousness is his definition of "person". For Sobrino, personhood is not gauged by the degree of self-knowledge one has of oneself. Rather, "personhood is ex-istence, a type of being that gets its consistency from another outside. . . . [that ultimately] realizes its existence either in dependence on God or in opposition to him."[68]

With this in mind, the first point Sobrino makes is that *"Jesus is aware of the fact that in and through his own person the kingdom of God is drawing near."*[69] This conclusion is based on the facts that Jesus verbally proclaimed the approaching kingdom and that he worked signs that indicated its approach. He performed miracles, forgave sins, and ate with sinners. He took an original and novel stance vis-à-vis the Law and the prophets. He began his teachings with "Amen," thereby asserting the truth of what followed rather than ending with it as a statement of faith. His parables spoke of the in-breaking of the kingdom, that is, salvation, in the present even though its consummation lay in the future.[70]

Sobrino's second point is that *"Jesus is bold enough to assert that eschatological salvation is determined by the stance a person adopts toward Jesus' own person."*[71] This should not be understood as a simple identification of Jesus with the future Son of Man; nor is it an assertion that Jesus understood himself ontologically as the Son of God. Sobrino is making the claim that *functionally* one's ultimate salvation or condemnation is dependent upon one's relationship to Jesus. In other words, one's acceptance of Jesus' message results in one's acceptance by the Son of Man, regardless of who the Son of Man is. Acceptance of Jesus' message is simply the following of him in service to God's kingdom.[72]

Sobrino's dynamic understanding of God's reign (God's actions reveal

God's being) is the basis for his discussion of Jesus' self-consciousness in relation to God. In keeping with his methodology, this relationship is revealed indirectly. The first clue is seen in Jesus' unconditional trust in God, as seen in his use of "Abba" to address Yahweh. "Abba" indicates an exclusive relationship with God in two ways. First, Jesus lived his life completely in and through God. His prayers are indicative of this point, especially those relating to the "fundamental moments" of his life. These moments reveal his sense of dependence upon God. Second, Jesus' relationship with God differs from that of other people as seen in his use of "my Father" and "your Father."[73]

The second clue is found in Jesus' unconditional obedience to God's will. Sobrino contends that Jesus' mission from God is so potent that it is an unspoken presupposition in the Synoptics. He goes so far as to say that "Jesus' life makes sense only in terms of his awareness of this mission."[74] Support for this statement is found in the Pauline and Johannine writings that speak of Jesus as one sent from God, and in the Letter to the Hebrews that describes this mission in terms of the Son's obedience.[75]

The Death of Jesus

Sobrino's approach to the death of Jesus is both traditional and unique. As previously noted, Sobrino accepts the historicity of Jesus' crucifixion; but he is critical of much of the church's reflection on the cross. His interpretation of this event is exegetically based, but he does not spend time analyzing the trials of Jesus, the method of crucifixion, or the texts that describe these events. He is concerned with the soteriological effect of the cross, but only in its relation to the rest of Jesus' life. What Sobrino offers is a theological interpretation of the crucifixion that includes certain traditional themes, but which also goes beyond them.

This is due to the fact that Latin Americans are beginning to see a continuity between Jesus' life and his death and resurrection. The cross cannot be separated from the concrete history of Jesus; nor can it be separated from God, given Jesus' fundamental relationships to God and God's kingdom. Finally, it cannot be separated from the Christian life, for it has a significant impact upon discipleship.[76] With this in mind, Sobrino interprets the cross of Jesus in terms of its significance for humanity, Jesus, and God.

For Sobrino, Jesus' death is best described by the word "scandal." More specifically, it is the scandal of God's abandonment of Jesus on the cross. This element of the crucifixion is preserved by Mark, Matthew, Paul, and the Letter to the Hebrews; but it seems that other New Testament writers found it difficult to reconcile this scandal with God's subsequent resurrection of Jesus from the dead. Luke and John present Jesus' death as triumphant and majestic. Further proof that this scandalous edge was dulled was the rise in the use of titles that reflect dignity: Messiah, Lord, and Son of God. Titles referring to Jesus' earthly work began to disappear, which is especially true for the title of Suffering Servant. According to Sobrino, this process of mollification caused the cross to recede into the background and to become a preliminary and provisional stage leading to the resurrection.[77]

The end result of this process is the reduction of the cross to a "noetic mystery" that is explicable in terms of God's eternal design for humanity, that is, salvation. Sobrino's criticism of this view lies in its presupposition that God's nature, and what constitutes divinity, is known prior to the crucifixion. He says:

> We cannot explain the cross *logically* by appealing to God, who supposedly is known already, because the first thing the cross does here is raise questions about God himself and the authentic reality of the deity.[78]

In other words, the cross raises questions about the nature of God, sin, and salvation. Tradition has done well in answering these questions on an interior, individualistic level. What is needed now are answers dealing with externalized injustice and sinfulness.[79]

Unfortunately, the history of theology reveals a continuance of this process of dehistoricization of the cross. The early church fathers did not take the scandal of the cross seriously because they conceived of God in terms of power rather than of love. The various theories of vicarious satisfaction which began with Anselm were also ahistorical in that they separated the cross from the history of Jesus.[80] In other words, reflection upon the cross was done backwards. The church's conception of God should have developed from the cross of Jesus. A corollary to this misguided methodology is the conception of worship as sacrifice. The cross became a religious symbol in a pejorative sense of the word. Once the cross was dehistoricized, worship replaced the actual following of Jesus.[81]

Sobrino's solution to this process is a startling one: an abandonment of Hellenistic metaphysics and epistemology. He contends that Greek philosophy was unable to contemplate nothingness, "the negative pole of reality." As long as the church utilizes this framework, a theology of the cross is impossible since the nothingness of death cannot be incorporated into God. If, however, one works from the cross to God, such a theology is possible. This will mean that suffering and death must be seen as a mode of existence for God, since historical love necessarily involves suffering. This is especially true if love is extended in, and to, a sinful world. For the Christian, God would not be God if, in the process of concretizing love within history, God remained unaffected by the misery caused by sin.[82]

Greek epistemology, based upon analogy and wonder, also invalidates any revelation of God in the cross of Jesus. The principle of analogy posits that like is known by like. Sobrino supplements analogy with the principle of dialectics. God is revealed in the cross as the one contradicting the world and its truth, not as the ultimate embodiment of transitory goodness and beauty. Wonder is the "trigger" that begins the search for the analogy between what is known and something new. Sobrino sharpens the concept of wonder with sorrow, a "highly qualified" type of wonder. Sorrow is the point of contact between Jesus' cross and all the other crosses of history. Caught between these two sets of crosses, sorrow issues forth in effective love by taking up the cross of Jesus in order to alleviate the suffering of others.[83]

To summarize, the significance of the cross for humanity has several aspects. First, the crucifixion is a scandal vis-à-vis Jesus' proclamation of God's kingdom drawing near in grace. Second, the cross of Jesus brings into question humanity's conception of God, how God is revealed, and what attitudes and actions mediate God's presence in history. Third, historical suffering and death is common both to humanity and to God. Finally, recognition of God in the cross of Jesus carries with it the call to discipleship, to offer oneself totally in service to the kingdom via the transformation of the world of human relationships.

The significance of the cross for Jesus himself is based on Sobrino's contention that the cross is the historical consequence of Jesus' life. Jesus proclaimed God's coming kingdom in a historical situation pervaded by sin. This sinfulness was not merely internal or individualistic; it also had an "external embodiment" that gave structure to personal sin. Thus, Jesus' proclamation brought him into conflict with the political and religious leaders of his day because he challenged their conception of God: Does God wield oppressive power (as embodied by the religious and political leaders) or does God offer and effect liberation (as embodied by Jesus)? The crisis evoked by the presentation of these two choices led Jesus to the cross. On the cross, both Jesus as the way to God and the God of Jesus is on trial.[84]

It follows from this that Jesus was crucified for his conception of God, that is, for blasphemy. More specifically, Jesus died for his conception of how to find access to God. God is not found in "privileged locales," such as the temple and worship. God is found among the poor and oppressed. The true God is a gracious and loving God who re-creates "the situation of every human being." The religious leaders of his day realized that Jesus was offering the people a choice: the God of Jesus or the God of the scribes and Pharisees.[85]

There was also a political aspect to Jesus' death, for he was crucified as a political agitator. Again, the issue at stake is what sort of power mediates God. Sobrino makes the interesting point that the Zealots were not rebuked the way other groups were. He notes that both Jesus and the Zealots wanted to establish God's kingdom; both felt that the kingdom was imminent. Jesus did not, however, espouse Zealot orthodoxy uncritically, for his conception of God differed from theirs: God would come in grace, and not via armed revolution. The destruction involved in revolution could not mediate a gracious God; therefore, Jesus conceived of God as love rather than power. This means love is political; it must take sides. Since God's love is being incarnated in a world pervaded by sin, "it can unfold and develop only by confronting the oppressive weight of power."[86] Since love is political, it must desacralize political power by taking the side of the oppressed.[87]

The cross as the historical consequence of Jesus' life also affects his call to discipleship. First, those answering his call must embody in their lives Jesus' own defense of the poor and prophetic denunciation of oppressive power structures. Second, by doing so, they will be enduring Christian suffering, for only the suffering that comes from following Jesus is Christian suffering. The first point means Christian spirituality is a political spirituality, for it is in the realm of politics that power is wielded. The second point provides the perspective from which the critique of religious and political idolatry derives.[88]

To summarize, the significance of the cross for Jesus is found in its continuation of his life's mission. First, God is partial to the poor and oppressed; any religious or political law that dehumanized people was denounced as sinful. Second, both the religious and political realms played a part in putting Jesus on the cross because he questioned their conceptions of God. Finally, following Jesus involves not only defending the poor and prophetically denouncing oppressive power structures, but it also means the disciple may be crucified like Jesus.

The significance of the cross of Jesus for God concerns the relationship between God and suffering. Jesus' suffering of crucifixion separates him from other martyrs because he died in "complete rupture" with his cause, abandoned by the very God he proclaimed. The basis for this rupture is Jesus' experience and proclamation of God as "Abba." The resurrection does not remove this scandal. In relation to the crucifixion, the resurrection only raises more questions about God's nature.[89]

The first step to be taken vis-à-vis God's true nature is a reformulation of transcendence. First, the cross of Jesus reveals God where natural theology, based on analogy, cannot find God. In fact, the God of natural theology is an idol, a contradiction of the true God. Second, God is not the one who wields power, but is the one who is subjected to the power of sin; God is revealed in suffering. This is why the oppressed are the "privileged mediation of God." Their very existence calls into question what it means to be human. This, in turn, is a question of the historical mediation of who God is. In traditional language, it is a question of theodicy with a slight modification. Ultimately, theodicy is a problem of God's relationship to suffering. Penultimately, that is, historically, it is "anthropocity," a question of justifying human beings and the history they have unleashed.[90] This leads directly to the second step necessary for a reconceptualization of God which derives from the cross.

The second step is a correct understanding of what took place on the cross. Simply put, "*on the cross of Jesus God himself is crucified.*"[91] This should not be understood simply as "God against God"; rather, it is the true God questioning the reality of an idol set up as God. On the cross, God suffers the death of the Son. In doing so, God takes upon Godself all of history's pain and suffering. A new future and a new hope is opened up for humankind out of history's "most negative side." This new future is based upon God's criticism of the world and upon God's ultimate solidarity with it.[92]

This historical concretion of love is dialectical; love is both active and passive. It is active in that it acts for the benefit of the ones loved. Love is passive in that it is situated in the world so that it is affected by injustice and death. On the cross, God is present for humanity but absent from Jesus. Within this dialectic of presence and absence, the love between God and Jesus is historicized by the Spirit's effecting of liberation in history.[93]

In this way, Sobrino offers a new understanding to the phrase, "saved by the cross." First, the cross reveals God's unconditional love within the bounds of history. The follower of Jesus is extended the invitation to be a "co-actor" with God in history by mediating God's love in a sinful situation. Second, to be saved by the cross means to participate in God's history of concretizing suffering love in history. To be sure, this is not an explanation of how the cross effects salvation; rather, it is an invitation to "experience history as salvation." In other words, salvation is meaningless if it is not historicized, that is, if it is seen merely as a private, interior experience.[94]

The cross is not God's last word on Jesus. Nor is resurrection God's last word on history, for God is not yet "all in all." Christian existence moves between the two poles of cross and resurrection. Sobrino summarizes this way of life in terms of the Pauline triad of faith, hope, and love. Faith in the God of Jesus is a "worldly" faith. It is always linked with the "mournful plaints of history": the cries of Israel in Egypt, Jesus' cry of dereliction from the cross, creation's groans of travail. Hope, like faith, is not ingenuous. Christians hope against injustice, oppression, and death. Christian hope is rooted in the cross of Jesus and in service to the crucified of history; it appears at the time when all seems hopeless. Love is also worldly because it is embodied in a world of sin and alienation as the basis for the re-structuring of persons and society, a structure whose goal is reconciliation.[95]

To summarize, the significance of the cross for God is two-fold. On the one hand, there is an intra-trinitarian restructuring of God; God becomes "personally" involved in the machinations of history and is personally affected by this involvement. On the other hand, humankind is permitted to participate in the very life of God, which participation does not do away with the mystery of God; rather, it is the way in which human beings respond to this mystery, that is, the way of the Son.

The Resurrection of Jesus

The raising of Jesus out of death is not, strictly speaking, a historical event, for no one witnessed it. Nor can one appeal to the empty tomb and "apparitions" of Jesus, for then historicity is based upon inference. Sobrino concludes from this that the resurrection is an "eschatological event" narrated as a "historical event." The resurrection is an eschatological event because:

> the revelation of God effected in Christ's resurrection is a promise. . . .
> because it is not a possibility *in* the world and *in* history but a possibility *for* the world and *for* history.[96]

As a promise, the resurrection is not something to be historically verified, but a mission to be carried out.[97] Therefore, the resurrection is not something to be proven, but an event to be understood and lived.

Sobrino posits three basic requisites for understanding the resurrection. They are "a radical hope in the future, a historical consciousness that grasps the meaning of history as a promise, and a specific praxis which is nothing else but the following of Jesus."[98] The first point is based upon the Jewish apocalyptic expectation of the end of time and of the re-creation of reality. This ultimate hope was expressed in the hope for the "resurrection of the dead," for resurrection implied a radically new situation that would be superior to the old one. When the disciples saw the apparitions of Jesus, they used the language of apocalypticism to describe what they saw: Jesus had been resurrected by God; but apocalyptic thought had to be reformed in light of what had happened to Jesus. Its core was not merely concerned with the end of time or with hope; it also included God's coming in grace. The hermeneutic for understanding the resurrection is not only hope, but also the search for justice. The difficulty in understanding the resurrection does not lie in how it occurred, but in whether or not God and the kingdom of God are like Jesus said they were. In other words, will justice triumph over injustice? Hope, therefore, can be a hermeneutical principle for understanding the resurrection only if it recognizes that the risen One is none other than the One who was crucified.[99]

The second point follows from the first. If hope is evoked by the resurrection of the crucified Jesus, the future must be seen as a promise; more specifically, it is the "definitive promise of God." It is more than the recognition of the open-endedness of history; it is a promise that the destiny of Jesus is the destiny of history and of all creation. As such, the resurrection is unfinished in regard to its saving efficacy. This means that the hope evoked by God's promise in Jesus' resurrection entails a mission.[100]

Sobrino's third point is the explication of that mission. Part of this mission involves what has been traditionally proclaimed vis-à-vis the resurrection: Jesus is the risen Christ. To this Sobrino adds praxis understood as following Jesus. As he says, "the resurrection sets in motion a life of service designed to implement in reality the eschatological ideals of justice, peace, and human solidarity."[101] This life must be concretized in the lives of the crucified peoples of history; that is to say, Christians are to proclaim, by word and deed, the good news of God's kingdom to the oppressed. When this is done, the resurrection will be a revelation of God's response to injustice. Thus, the resurrection symbolizes, indirectly and proleptically, the ultimate triumph of justice.[102]

The ultimate triumph of justice leads directly to another modification that Sobrino makes in regard to the traditional understanding of Jesus' resurrection, that is, the resurrection as a way of dealing with death. Sobrino contends that how one deals with one's own death coincides with how one deals with the death of others, especially of those people who have been killed by the oppression of others. Belief and hope in the resurrection as one's own future is based upon one's participation in the overcoming of injustice. The attitude necessary to keep this hope from becoming self-centered is to take:

> as absolutely scandalous the death of the crucified today . . . [an attitude] which must not be allowed ultimately to become something secondary in one's own interests in virtue of a hope in one's own resurrection.[103]

In other words, to gain one's life one must lose it, either in service to the oppressed or in actual death resulting from that service.[104]

The conclusion that one is forced to draw from this is both simple and hard: "resurrection is for the crucified."[105] This statement should not be understood as a negation of the offer of salvation to all of humankind; but it does reveal the "correct lens" through which one must view this universal offer. The poor have always experienced death at the hands of self-centered power structures. In this way their death is analogous to the death of Jesus and is the basis of their hope in the resurrection. But what about the people who are not poor and are not so obviously oppressed? The answer is pro-existence, in living for others. If one's death results from service rendered to the poor, one's death is analogous to the death of Jesus. In this way one shares in crucifixion and, consequently, in the hope for resurrection.106

For Sobrino, Jesus' resurrection impacts God, humanity, and Jesus himself. The "theological meaning" of the resurrection has several aspects. First, God is defined in terms of action, as in the Old Testament, rather than in terms of "*properties*," as in "Hellenic essentialism." Second, God's actions in the present do not negate God's futurity. The resurrection of Jesus is "the definitive *promise* of God." Third, God's "*activity* in the resurrection" must be balanced with "God's *passivity* on the cross." The resurrection is the other side of the cross, not a separate event. Fourth, God is revealed by God's "resurrection of the crucified" one, that is, by God's "*fidelity*" to Jesus in this event. Finally, God's fidelity to Jesus in this two-sided event makes the assertion that "God is love" possible. Together, the cross and resurrection reveal God's powerful love or loving power.107

The "soteriological meaning" of the resurrection has two aspects: reconciliation and a "liberative future." The former includes both humanity's relationship to God and human relationships. Reconciliation is possible because it is "costly grace." As Sobrino says: "There is reconciliation because there was love; and there was love because there was suffering and death."108 Thus, "love is creative," that is, it creates a new relationship with God which forms the basis for a transformation of human relationships. These new relationships imply a liberative future for humankind, that is, a universal resurrection. Hence, the resurrection is not merely a "past event" nor the authentication of the present; it orients humanity toward the future in a way that transforms the present.109

The "christological meaning" of the resurrection culminates in the confession: "Jesus is the Son of God." Sobrino is indebted to Leonardo Boff's "christological process" for his explication of this process.110 Sobrino, however, does not merely paraphrase Boff; he also has his own concerns. First, Sobrino emphasizes the "structural feature of anticipation" in the life of Jesus, who proclaimed the approach of God's kingdom. Thus, the people's relationship to Jesus determines their "*future* salvation or condemnation." This future orientation is also seen in: 1) the "personal" oneness of Jesus with the Son of Man; and 2) the phrase "Maranatha," with its expectation of Jesus' coming again. Second, Sobrino stresses the tension that exists between the "future parousia" of Jesus and the presence of the exalted Lord in cultic worship. The problem arises not in the recognition of this tension, but in the tendency to subordinate the former to the latter. For Sobrino, both are necessary for a proper understanding of the "figure of Jesus." Sobrino's third concern is trinitarian. Jesus' divinity derives from his relationship with the Father. More specifically, it is seen in the way he historically concretized his trust in, and surrender to, the Father. Finally, Sobrino calls for new titles to signify Jesus' meaning for today. Sobrino finds some of these titles in

Scripture. "Servant of Yahweh" should be revived and paired with "Lord" in order to explicate fully the "sovereignty of Christ" and to concretize the idea of "power" in Christian terms. Because of their "distinctiveness" vis-à-vis the divine-human relationship, the christological implications of phrases such as "Christ crucified" and "slain lamb" should not be overlooked. As expected, Sobrino includes "Liberator" among the possiblities. He issues one caveat concerning the construction of new titles: Jesus himself determines the appropriateness and content of the title that is attributed to him. If the reverse occurs, the "christological concentration of theology" begins to erode.[111]

Dogma and Christology

The christological dogma of Chalcedon is one of the possible starting points that Sobrino rejects. This rejection is not equivalent to a rejection of its validity as dogma; but, as dogma, it must be interpreted before it can be meaningful.

Dogma: Role and
Definition

Before any dogma can be meaningful, its function must be correctly understood. For Sobrino, dogma performs two roles. First, dogma defends some aspect of the faith which is perceived to be under attack. This is accomplished by crystalizing the essential elements necessary for an orthodox belief. Therefore, dogma is dependent upon what has already been preached and taught. Second, dogma attempts to provide a better understanding of Scripture. It does this by using the language and concepts familiar to those embroiled in conflict.[112]

By describing the role of dogma in this way, Sobrino does several things. First, he goes beyond a mere etymological understanding of the word as "opinion" or "resolution." He also stops short of the modern connotation of dogma as giving voice to the depths of Christian faith.[113] The third thing he does is point out the limitations of dogma: 1) dogma always says less than Scripture says, that is, it does not exhaust its subject; and 2) the passing of time calls for the interpretation of dogma because the crisis has passed, but the truth of the dogmatic statement remains.[114]

With this in mind, Sobrino defines dogma as "a doxological statement in which we seek to formulate the mysterious reality of God himself."[115] To understand this definition, it is necessary to know the difference between doxological statements and historical statements. The latter are statements about God in relation to a historical event; they are indirect statements about God. The former are statements about God in and of Godself; they are direct statements about the very essence of God. From a human perspective, God cannot be known directly; therefore, doxological statements must be based upon historical statements.[116] It follows from this that christological dogmas, as doxological statements, must be based upon historical statements about Christ; and what is known of Christ's historical life is found in the presentation of the historical Jesus in the Gospels.

Reinterpretation of Chalcedon

Sobrino's reinterpretation of Chalcedon is more concerned with methodology than with content. As he says:

> An authentically orthodox Christology must end up with the ontological affirmation of the Incarnation. Epistemologically, however, it must work in the opposite direction.[117]

In other words, Christology must begin with the historical Jesus and end with the confession that this Jesus is the Son of God. In light of this, Sobrino makes three negative comments about Chalcedon's dogma. First, Chalcedon's language lacks concreteness--the definitions of "God" and "man" are assumed to be known and applied to Jesus and his God. Sobrino contends that this is christologically backward, that is, the content of these terms can be known only on the basis of Christ. Second, the statements of Chalcedon lack historicity. The Incarnation is defined statically in terms of "nature" and "person"; the historical life and ministry of Jesus are not mentioned. Third, little is to be found concerning relationality. Statements about Jesus' being the Son are present, evidently due to the relationship between Jesus and the Logos; but in the Synoptics, Jesus' sonship is based upon his relationship with "Abba."[118] In other words, the basic problem is that the dogma of Chalcedon contains no historical statements, no references to Jesus of Nazareth; hence, no historical foundation for its faith statements.

The positive attributes of Chalcedon become evident when it is seen as a doxological statement with the history of Jesus as its foundation. When viewed in this light, Chalcedon functions as a limit-statement, which sets the boundaries for every other ecclesial Christology. This does not mean the formula of Chalcedon is the beginning and the end of Christology, for its historical nature will not allow this; but it does highlight its part of the process in trying to understand who Jesus Christ is.[119]

Second, the divinity of Christ is known "indirectly" through the history of Jesus. The only way one can comprehend Christ's divinity (in itself unknowable by humanity) is by the way it is lived out within the bounds of history. This is another example of Sobrino's use of relationality. Jesus lived his life in "radical surrender" to God, a lifestyle characterized by his confidence in God and obedience to his mission of proclaiming God's kingdom; Jesus lived for the other (God), not himself. This lifestyle was confirmed by the resurrection. Thus, a special relationship was formed between Jesus and God, one Sobrino calls "filiation."[120] The doxological statement that Jesus is the Eternal Son comes about "when we identify Jesus' historical filiation with the eternal filiation of the Son."[121]

The Historical Jesus and
the Christ of Faith

Sobrino's choice to focus his Christology on the historical Jesus is an implicit recognition of a tension in theology between the historical Jesus and the risen Christ. He contends that:

> *whenever Christian faith focuses one-sidedly on the Christ of faith and wittingly or unwittingly forgets the historical Jesus, and to the extent that it does, it loses its specific structure as Christian faith and tends to turn into religion.*[122]

This is not a question of either-or, but of priority. According to Sobrino:

> access to the Christ of faith can only come through access to the historical Jesus, through discipleship. . . . [for] the Christ of faith is . . . the very man who lived a certain kind of life and died a certain way because of that.[123]

Whether or not one adheres to this prioritization will affect the way one views the relationship between Jesus' cross and resurrection, faith and dogma, power and its use, and worship and discipleship.[124]

Cross and Resurrection

For Sobrino, the church in Corinth describes a one-sided view of the resurrection and the risen Christ. It stresses the enthronement of Jesus as Lord of the cosmos. Christians are already in heaven; the future is already present. There is an emphasis upon Christ's presence in the community: the historical Jesus has almost disappeared. Union with Christ is accomplished by partaking of the sacraments.[125]

Paul's reaction was a return to the "most concrete and scandalous" aspect of Jesus' life: his cross. The cross is not the gateway to resurrection; rather, it is the other side of resurrection. Christ's present Lordship is incomplete because injustice still exists. The sacraments are pro-existent; they exist to build up the community. Christian faith is not worship and triumphant enthusiasm; it is following Jesus. The freedom of the resurrection is actually the freedom of the cross: to serve others and suffer, as Jesus did, because of that service. Worship follows discipleship rather than replaces it.[126]

Faith and Dogma

A one-sided interpretation of the risen Christ as explicative Logos represents the move from faith as discipleship to faith as the explanation of reality. This process began in the New Testament with the gradual shift in emphasis from Christology to ecclesiology. Since the church presumed to possess the truth about Jesus, it began to formulate conceptions that turned faith into doctrines. In the second step, Christian faith became a religion with faith being the first step in the way of "Christianity." The process continued as Christianity adopted religious terms to describe itself. Faith became piety, a virtue directed solely toward the deity. The Apologists, having to defend the notion that faith was real knowledge, completed this process by turning faith into a "theory of Christianity," that is, a set of doctrines that were logical, and that logically explained reality.127

According to Sobrino, the basic error of this line of thought is its forgetting of Jesus of Nazareth, its forgetting that the wisdom of God is found in the cross. The wisdom of the cross defines the Christian theory of reality: it is explicative and critical. The Christian's Logos is one who was crucified and resurrected; he depicts a God different from human religious perceptions. The God of this Logos criticizes history from within. Mere cognitive faith, based upon an explicative Logos, is inadequate. It must be coupled with critical and practical theories that take into account the life of Jesus.128

Power and Its Use

In antiquity, the state and religion were interdependent. Power, associated with the deity, was mediated by the state. Religion provided ideological support for the state. This is what happened in the Roman Empire and Christianity. The process by which Christianity moved from an illicit religion to the religion of the Empire is well known and need not be reviewed here. Suffice it to say, the result of that process turned faith in Jesus into a state religion. Sobrino notes that this was facilitated by a "specific notion of Christian universalism": the church had a mission that pertained to the whole world; but its ultimate theological reason was a one-sided understanding of the risen Lord as one who wields power. This view of the Lord's power, however, was not based upon the praxis of the historical Jesus. The political theology that became the state religion was based on the belief that society would last only as long as it remained submissive to the totalitarian power of the state.129

Sobrino advocates another interpretation of the risen Lord as one who wields power, a way based upon the historical Jesus. In his life and death, Jesus desacralized power. For him, God's power was found in the weak and the powerless. It was a power exercised through the "praxis of discipleship." Negatively, this entails prophetic denunciation. Positively, it means the attempt to organize society based upon the justice preached by Jesus. Together, these two points allow for provisional embodiments of God's kingdom, embodiments whose form is dependent upon the situation at hand.130

Worship and Discipleship

The tension between worship and discipleship began in the Hellenistic Christian communities. The catalyst was a growing focus upon Christ as the exalted Lord present in worship. The Lord's Supper came to be viewed as a sacrifice, while the preached word began to decline in importance. With this new understanding of the liturgy came a more cultic view of the community's leadership. Distinctions were made between sacred and profane, clergy and laity, and bishops and priests. Worship became the way to gain access to God and Christ. The church saw itself as the mediator of salvation. In other words, cultic worship took precedence over everything, especially discipleship.[131]

For Sobrino, the relationship between worship and discipleship should be the inverse of the previous situation; worship flows out of discipleship. His reasoning is based upon the Christology of the Letter to the Hebrews, in which Jesus is called by God to be a priest. But for that author, Jesus defines what it means to be a priest; Jesus does not offer sacrifices, he offers himself. He does not operate in the realm of the sacred, but in the realm of history. His mediation was an advocacy of love and justice among human beings. As the exalted Lord, Jesus ought to be acclaimed; but worship alone does not give access to God. Only when it is preceded by the following of Jesus, by advocating justice and love, can worship have any meaning.[132]

To summarize, Sobrino contends that the correct way to view the relationship between cross and resurrection, faith and the faith, power and its use, and worship and discipleship is through the lens of the historical Jesus. First, the revelation of God in history is seen in relation to the cries of oppressed people. Access to God, that is, one's response to this revelation, is to give oneself in service to the oppressed. Second, history is not fixed from the beginning; rather, it is something to be fashioned "along the way." Third, the following of Jesus is both grace and responsibility. It is grace in that it reflects God's ultimate solidarity with humanity, and that God's ultimate goal, for all creation, is reconciliation. Following Jesus is a responsibility in that human beings are called to incarnate God's love in a world pervaded by sin.

Christology in Sobrino's Theology

Throughout his writings, Sobrino has touched upon all the subject areas of theology, but he seems to focus upon three in particular: God, the church, and the Christian life. Not coincidentally, his Christology has had a major impact on all three.

Sobrino makes the surprising claim that God is not ultimate for Jesus, because:

> to state that God is [ultimate for Jesus] would be equivalent to saying that what is ultimate for Jesus is not essentially related to history and that history is not essentially related to it.[133]

God can be ultimate for Jesus only if God is known as the God of the kingdom. This reflects two of Sobrino's basic methodological points. First, God is known indirectly through God's liberative acts in history. The second point deals with relationships. God is revealed through Jesus' proclamation, in word and deed, of God's coming kingdom. From these two points, Sobrino concludes that God is transcendent, omnipotent, and that God is a God of life.

God's actions in history reveal God to be transcendent, greater than anything human; but this transcendent God is a God of grace, capable of realizing the unimaginable, that is, the transformation of sinful human beings and their world. For Sobrino, this means that the essence of God's transcendence is love, which is not an abstract love. It expresses itself within the vicissitudes of history; it is a partisan love for the poor and oppressed. That God is love has three corollaries. First, God does not claim any "rights" for Godself that are detrimental to human beings. Second, service to God by human beings be of service to others.134   Third, love between human beings is a mediation of God's transcendence, for it equates living with living for others.135

Sobrino's God is also omnipotent, although this is not evident at first. The credibility of God's power involves both Jesus' crucifixion and resurrection, impotence and power. Paradoxically, God's impotence lends credibility to the notion of God's power in the resurrection because this helplessness "is the expression of God's absolute nearness to the poor, sharing their lot to the end."136 Without this "catch," God's power would remain ambiguous and, for the world's crucified, historically threatening. Only as an expression of love is God's power made credible. Once God's presence on the cross is verified, God's power is felt as salvific, as confirmation of the hope that justice will ultimately triumph over injustice.137

Therefore, God is a God of life. God's "archetypal plan" for humanity is life. The first mediation of this plan is creation itself. In creation, God created life and the resources necessary for its maintenance.138 The Law is another mediation of God's will for life. It provided the basis for respect of life, whatever form it may take: parents, neighbor, sojourner, widow, or orphan. This understanding of the Law forms the basis for Jesus' anathemas against the religious leaders of his day. Any interpretation of the Law that took away the necessities of life was denounced because it came from a false divinity, not the God of life.139

The impact of Sobrino's Christology upon his ecclesiology is seen in two ways. The first is his view of the objective and subjective witness of the Church. The Church's objective witness is to a "just life in the presence of death." Theologically, the Church bears witness to Jesus, his proclamation of God's kingdom, his partisan love for the poor, and of God as the God of life and liberation. Historically, this witness is active participation in the struggle against injustice. In other words, the objective witness of the Church is a praxis based upon following Jesus; therefore, it entails conflict. It will involve the Church in events that are gray, rather than black and white. The Church will participate in these events with groups and organizations that it often criticizes. This is inevitable if the Church is to have a voice in the structuring of a more just life; but it is also the Church's recovery of the way Jesus met people and their needs: he fed them, healed them, and prayed that they might have the basic necessities of life. He unmasked and denounced the hypocrisy of the existing power structures in defense of the poor and oppressed.140

The subjective witness that flows from this is "persecution leading to martyrdom."141 This persecution differs from the Church's past persecutions because it comes from the hands of people who give *prima facie* allegiance to the

Christian faith. This persecution has two forms. The Church is persecuted when its people, clergy or laity, are threatened, harassed, or killed in their mission to concretize justice and integral liberation. The Church is also persecuted when any life is threatened. To be sure, this is an indirect persecution of the Church; but it is no less real for it is an attack upon the kingdom of God and, therefore, a persecution of the God whom the Church serves. This two-pronged view of persecution has three results. First, the Church will not accept any form of persecution. Second, the Church will become more sensitive to the various forms persecution takes. Third, the Church will learn who the poor are, what solidarity with the poor really entails, and more about its own nature as ex-istence.[142]

Another way Sobrino's Christology affects his ecclesiology revolves around the idea of solidarity. From this perspective, Sobrino re-defines the Church's catholicity and mission and re-directs the focus of ecumenical activity. Solidarity re-defines catholicity as a co-responsibility of churches for one another in sharing with one another in all areas of life. In other words, it is the gift of faith to faith, of churches sharing with one another the diversity of the one faith. This idea is actually carried out in the sending of "missionaries" from a First World Church to one in the Third World. There is a mutual giving and receiving in this process, for the faith of both churches is strengthened and expanded by the experiences of those who are first sent to serve and then re-sent to tell of their work. All of this presupposes that some local churches are in solidarity with the poor. And it is this presupposition that underlies Sobrino's view of ecumenism. The fundamental unity of the Church is its solidarity with the poor, its faith in favor of life for human beings. Sobrino contends there can be no hope for any other type of "interconfessional" unity without this fundamental unity.[143]

Sobrino calls the church that bears this witness "the church of the poor." The poor, who constitute the historical and social basis of this church, are poor due to their impoverishment by others; therefore, the church of the poor gives "preferential attention" to the poor, for they are the most deprived of life. This means the poor are the "hermeneutical principle" by which the church of the poor understands basic Christian concepts and realities.[144]

Sobrino's view of the Christian life is greatly influenced by his Christology, a fact already evident in the discussion above of "Jesus of Nazareth." Simply put, discipleship is nothing but "the task of historically reproducing Jesus' own history."[145] First, discipleship is solidarity with the poor by proclaiming the good news of God's kingdom, by defending their cause, by struggling against injustice, and by accepting the consequences of that advocacy.[146] Second, discipleship recognizes Jesus as the "firstborn" of faith. Following Jesus acknowledges that he has been revealed as the Son of God. It also acknowledges this revelation as the revelation of the way to God, of the way to become a child of God. Jesus has already lived the life of faith to the end, clearing the path for others to follow. From this perspective, the difference between Jesus and his disciples is historical rather than ontological.[147]

Notes

[1]Biographical information was gleaned from the following sources: Jon Sobrino, *Christology at the Crossroads: A Latin American Approach*, trans. John Drury (Maryknoll: Orbis Books, 1978), cited hereafter as *Christology*; *The True Church and the Poor*, trans. Matthew J. O'Connell (Maryknoll: Orbis Books, 1984), cited hereafter as *True Church*; *Resurrección de la Verdadera Iglesia: Los Pobres, lugar teológico de la eclesiología*, 2nd ed. (Santander, Spain: Editorial Sal Terre, 1984); *Romero: Martyr for Liberation* (London: Catholic Institute for International Relations, 1982); Deane William Ferm, *Third World Liberation Theologies: An Introductory Survey* (Maryknoll: Orbis Books, 1986), p. 125 and Ferm, *Profiles in Liberation: 36 Portraits of Third World Theologians* (Mystic, Connecticut: Twenty-Third Publications, 1988), pp. 184-87.

[2]Jon Sobrino, *Jesus in Latin America* (Maryknoll: Orbis Books, 1987), p. 3. Cited hereafter as *Jesus*.

[3]Sobrino, *Christology*, p. xx.   [4]Ibid., p. xxi.   [5]Ibid., pp. xxi-xxiii.

[6]Ibid., p. xxiv. Sobrino agrees with Wolfhart Pannenberg and Jürgen Moltmann on the trinitarian nature of Christology. See Wolfhart Pannenberg, *Jesus--God and Man*, 2nd ed. trans. Lewis L. Wilkins and Duane A. Priebe (Philadelphia: Westminster Press, 1977), pp. 115-83, esp. pp. 158-60 and 179-83. Cited hereafter as *Jesus*. See also Jürgen Moltmann, *The Crucified God: The Cross of Christ as the Foundation and Criticism of Christian Theology*, trans. R. A. Wilson and John Bowden (New York: Harper & Row, 1974), pp. 235-49: "Trinitarian Structure of the Cross." Cited hereafter as *Crucified God*.

[7]Sobrino, *Christology*, p. xxiv.   [8]Ibid., pp. xxiii-xxv.   [9]Ibid., p. 3.

[10]Ibid., pp. 3-8.   [11]Ibid.   [12]Ibid., p. 3.   [13]Ibid., pp. 9-13.

[14]Sobrino, *Jesus*, pp. 73-74.   [15]Ibid., p. 77.

[16]Ibid., p. 74. See Edward Schillebeeckx, *Jesus: An Experiment in Christology*, trans. Herbert Hoskins (New York: Crossroad, 1981), pp. 81-102.

[17]Sobrino, *Jesus*, p. 74.

[18]Sobrino, *Christology*, pp. 18-21.   Sobrino applied these guideposts to the Christologies of Karl Rahner, Wolfhart Pannenberg, and Jürgen Moltmann. This served two purposes. First, they were test cases for the validity of his hermeneutic. Second, it allowed him to show some general continuities and discontinuities between his Latin American Christology and contemporary European Christologies that also hearken back to the historical Jesus (pp. 22-33).

[19]Sobrino, *Jesus*, p. 143.   [20]Sobrino, *Christology*, pp. 33-37.   [21]Ibid., p. 41.

[22]Ibid., pp. 60-61.

23Sobrino distilled these elements from the summary of Jesus' preaching found in Mark 1:15: "The time is fulfilled, and the kingdom of God is at hand; repent, and believe in the gospel" (RSV).

24Sobrino, *Jesus*, pp. 89-90.   25Ibid., p. 143.   26Ibid., p. 108.   27Ibid., p. 86.

28Sobrino, *Christology*, p. 43.

29Ibid., p. 44. Here, again, relationality is evident. God and humanity work together to establish the kingdom, even though it remains God's kingdom.

30Ibid., pp. 44-45. This conclusion is also another example of Sobrino's use of relationality, but in the form of indirectness. Who God is, in and of Godself, cannot be known directly; but God's essence can be safely inferred from God's acts in history; doxological statements are based upon historical statements.

31Sobrino, *Christology*, p. 46.   32Ibid., pp. 46-47.   33Ibid., p. 47.   34Ibid.

35Ibid., p. 48.   36Ibid., pp. 48-49.

37Ibid., p. 50. So Jesus preaches the kingdom as grace, opening up the only future left to the oppressed. If they accept his offer, they are pardoned, that is, they recognize the fact that God is drawing near in grace. Rejection of Jesus' offer results in condemnation.

38Sobrino, *Christology*, pp. 51-53.   39Ibid., pp. 54-55.   40Ibid., p. 57.

41Ibid. In this attitude, conversion softens the scandal of particularity but does not do away with it. The kingdom is for the poor, who are in their state because of oppression, which everyone experiences. Therefore, the kingdom is for all people even though it is offered first to the poor.

42Sobrino, *Christology*, pp. 57-59.

43Ibid., p. 59. This is Sobrino's version of how the proclaimer became the proclaimed. The "proclamation of Jesus" is not primarily a doxological statement. He is proclaimed because he reveals the way, the process, by which one becomes a child of God.

44Ibid., pp. 59-60. Taken together, these two points reveal the difference between knowing about conversion and experiencing conversion. It is impossible for one to hear the call of discipleship in Jesus' proclamation of God's kingdom without radically altering one's attitudes and actions.

45Sobrino, *Christology*, p. 85.   46Ibid., p. 87.   47Ibid., pp. 91-92.   48Ibid., p. 93.

49Ibid., pp. 93-94.   50Ibid., pp. 94-95.   51Ibid., pp. 96-97.   52Ibid., pp. 97-98.

53Ibid., p. 98.

54Ibid., p. 99. Sobrino's view of Jesus' death is examined in detail below, pp. 137-48.

55Sobrino, *Christology*, pp. 99-100. Sobrino concluded that idolatry was an issue in Gethsemane because Jesus had to choose either the God of the kingdom he had proclaimed or the god that ruled with oppressive power. For an amplification of this view, see Sobrino, *Jesus*, pp. 98-128.

56Sobrino, *Christology*, p. 100.   57Cf. Mark 9:1, 13:22, 13:30; and Matthew 10:23.

58Sobrino, *Christology*, pp. 100-02. Jesus' "theological ignorance" is another way Sobrino states his case for Jesus' being the way to God. "Way" is understood as a road to be traveled, not as the means by which one is carried to God; thus, the humanity of Jesus is an example of pro-existence. The Incarnation was not merely the means to attain the end of human salvation. God's becoming flesh and tabernacling in the midst of humanity expresses God's love for, and solidarity with, humankind. In other words, by living the way he did, Jesus revealed the way in which human beings are to live with one another and with God. Following this way is verification of Jesus' person and message, of the in-breaking of God's kingdom, and of authentic liberation.

59Ibid., pp. 104-07.

60Sobrino, *Christology*, pp. 147-51. The prayers Jesus criticized are found in Matthew 6:5; 7:8; 7:21; Mark 12:38,40; Luke 9:29; 18:11. Sobrino said the accounts of Jesus' baptism and transfiguration emphasize his being "at prayer" and not the miraculous phenomena surrounding those events.

61Ibid., pp. 151-52.

62Ibid., p. 154. This prayer fulfills the characteristics of true prayer as stated above. It is completely other oriented. Jesus' words are directed to God and are a thanksgiving for God's work among the poor. In an indirect way, it is a petition on behalf of the oppressed to continue to be open to the work of God in their midst. This prayer also reflects the humility of Jesus as the servant of the kingdom. Jesus himself does not accomplish this work; God reveals Godself through his proclamation. Finally, this prayer shows Jesus' intent to do God's will. This goes back to Sobrino's idea that the goal of the kingdom is the total transformation of reality, a transformation that is first and foremost good news for the poor.

63Sobrino, *Christology*, p. 157.

64Ibid., pp. 155-57. This prayer, too, fits the characteristics of true prayer. The most obvious aspect is Jesus' searching for God's will at a time of great personal crisis. As in the first prayer, God's will was expressed in unexpected ways. Closely related to this is the fact that it was other oriented. It was primarily directed toward God and only secondarily concerned with Jesus' own actions. In its being directed to God, it was indirectly concerned with others, for it related to his proclamation of God's kingdom to the oppressed. Finally, this prayer reveals Jesus' humility before God. He did not bargain or manipulate; he simply offered himself to God.

65Clark M. Williamson, "Christ Against the Jews: A Review of Jon Sobrino's Christology," *Encounter*, 40 (1979), 410.

66Sobrino, *Christology*, p. 159. Sobrino is indebted to Pannenberg for this concept. See Wolfhart Pannenberg, *Basic Questions in Theology: Collected Essays*, Vol. I, trans. George H. Kehn (Philadelphia: Fortress Press, 1970), pp. 211-38. See also Wolfhart Pannenberg et al., eds., *Revelation as History*, trans. David Granskou (New York: Macmillan Company, 1968), pp. 125-31. Cited hereafter as *Revelation*.

67Sobrino, *Christology*, pp. 159-74.   68Ibid., p. 73. Cf. n. 24 above.

69Ibid., p. 68.   70Ibid., pp. 68-69.   71Ibid., p. 69.

72Ibid., pp. 69-70. Cf. Pannenberg, *Jesus*, p. 107: "The important thing in [Mark 8:38] is the material correspondence of the coming judgment with the present attitude of men toward Jesus."

73Sobrino, *Christology*, p. 71.   74Ibid., p. 72.   75Ibid., pp. 71-72.

76Ibid., pp. 180-81.

77Ibid., pp. 184-86. Cf. Moltmann, *Crucified God*, pp. 235-49, esp. pp. 241-44. Moltmann's influence is evident in Sobrino's emphasis upon suffering and death as a mode of God's existence because God is love; Jesus' abandonment on the cross by the Father; abandonment as a "rupture" between Jesus and the God of love he proclaimed; and the cross as an intratrinitarian "event" between the Father and the Son.

78Sobrino, *Christology*, p. 188.   79Ibid., pp. 187-90.   80Ibid., pp. 191-93.

81Ibid., p. 194. Except for these examples, Sobrino did not interact with the classical theories of atonement. It seems they are all "ahistorical," i.e., they begin with God's "eternal plan" rather than the history of Jesus. Therefore, he does not advocate any of them. The closest he comes to a "classical" theory is that of "the crucified God."

82Sobrino, *Christology*, pp. 195-97. Cf. Moltmann, *Crucified God*, pp. 227, 230, and 248 among many.

83Sobrino, *Christology*, pp. 198-200.

84Ibid., pp. 202-04. Cf. Moltmann, *Crucified God*, pp. 149-51.

85Sobrino, *Christology*, pp. 204-09. Cf. Moltmann, *Crucified God*, pp. 128-35.

86Sobrino, *Christology*, p. 214. Cf. Moltmann, *Crucified God*, pp. 136-45.

87Sobrino, *Christology*, pp. 211-14. For a more detailed analysis of political love, see Jon Sobrino, *Spirituality of Liberation: Toward Political Holiness*, trans. Robert R. Barr (Maryknoll: Orbis Books, 1988), pp. 80-86. Cited hereafter as *Spirituality*.

88Sobrino, *Christology*, pp. 215-16. Idolatry is an issue because a god of power is not the God of the kingdom. Cf. Moltmann, *Crucified God*, pp. 317-38: "The Political Liberation of Man."

[89]Sobrino, *Christology*, pp. 217-19. Cf. Moltmann, *Crucified God*, pp. 145-53, esp. pp. 146-51.

[90]Sobrino, *Christology*, pp. 219-24.

[91]Ibid., p. 224. Cf. Moltmann, *Crucified God*, pp. 151-52, and 245-49. But Sobrino adds new insights to those of Moltmann.

[92]Sobrino, *Christology*, pp. 224-25.   [93]Ibid., p. 226.   [94]Ibid., pp. 226-27.

[95]Ibid., pp. 229-33.   [96]Ibid., p. 252.   [97]Ibid., p. 253.   [98]Ibid., p. 256.

[99]Ibid., pp. 241-45.   [100]Ibid., pp. 251-53.   [101]Ibid., p. 255.

[102]Sobrino, *Jesus*, p. 149. Cf. Sobrino, *Christology*, pp. 255-56: First, this mission "must be political." It takes into consideration the modern situation, which in this case, is injustice and oppression. Thus, this mission must be open to new forms of concretization. Second, this mission must derive from "the theology of the cross." It must take into account the power of "evil and injustice." Finally, this mission is a mission of hope because it seeks to transform the cosmos, including all human reality.

[103]Sobrino, *Christology*, p. 151.   [104]Ibid., p. 150.   [105]Ibid., p. 152.

[106]Ibid., pp. 151-52.   [107]Ibid., pp. 260-61.   [108]Ibid., p. 262.

[109]Ibid., pp. 262-64.

[110]Ibid., pp. 264 and 272, n. 12. Cf. Leonardo Boff, *Jesus Christ Liberator: A Critical Christology for our Time*, trans. Patrick Hughes (Maryknoll: Orbis Books, 1978), pp. 139-77 and 226-46.

[111]Sobrino, *Christology*, pp. 264-72.   [112]Ibid., pp. 317-18.   [113]Ibid., pp. 313-16.

[114]Ibid., p. 318.   [115]Ibid., p. 323.

[116]Ibid. Sobrino's view of the role and definition of dogma has done more than elucidate the dogmatic process. It has reinforced the role of history for the construction of Christology. Time and space, economics and politics, and society and religion play major roles in defining culture and being human. Jesus, and anyone who desires to follow him, must interact with, and even confront, these realities. It has also expanded the role of relationality in Christology. To be alive means to be in relationship with other people, God, *and* cultural structures. To know who Jesus was (and is) one must properly understand his nexus of relationships within his culture and, also, the import it has for one's own relationships.

[117]Sobrino, *Christology*, p. 339.   [118]Ibid., pp. 329-31.   [119]Ibid., pp. 333-35.

[120]Ibid., pp. 336. Sobrino combined Augustine's concept of the social Trinity and Richard of St. Victor's definition of person as ex-istence for his line of reasoning.

121Sobrino, *Christology*, p. 337.   122Ibid., p. 275.   123Ibid.

124See also ibid., pp. 275-78: Sobrino also expressed this tension as the tension between faith and religion. He defined the latter as "a conception of reality, in which the meaning of the whole is always given at the start because the reality of God is satisfactorily shaped and defined from the very beginning" (p. 275). According to "religion," God is omnipotent, omniscient, and retributive justice. Anthropology is defined in terms of the past rather than the future; history is superfluous. Access to the deity is through the privileged locales such as worship or reason. The deity is totally transcendent but manipulable through the fulfillment of legalistic and moralistic requirements. Through them, worshipers can secure themselves against a totally demanding deity. Christian faith, on the other hand, contends that the essence of God appears at the end of time. God acts within history to transform it rather than to explain or justify it. The classical concepts of divinity are fleshed out in terms of grace and love. The meaning of history cannot be ascertained until injustice is eradicated. Security vis-à-vis the Christian God is assured by giving oneself totally to God. Access to God comes indirectly through service to others, especially the poor and oppressed. This fulfillment of Christian obligations verifies one's participation in God's life. Cf. Wolfhart Pannenberg, *Theology and the Kingdom of God*, trans. Richard John Neuhaus (Philadelphia: Westminster Press, 1969), pp. 56-58; also p. 63: "God is in himself the power of the future. . . . He is the ultimate future." See also Pannenberg, *Revelation*, pp. 131-35 and Wolfhart Pannenberg, "Constructive and Critical Functions of Christian Eschatology," *Harvard Theological Review*, 77 (1984), 123-25.

125Sobrino, *Christology*, pp. 279-80.   126Ibid., pp. 280-82.

127Ibid., pp. 287-91.   128Ibid., p. 291.   129Ibid., pp. 292 and 298.

130Ibid., pp. 293 and 298.   131Ibid., pp. 300-02.

132Ibid., pp. 302-04.   133Sobrino, *Jesus*, p. 83.

134Sobrino, *Christology*, pp. 163-69.   135Sobrino, *Jesus*, pp. 124-25.

136Ibid., p. 153.   137Ibid.

138Jon Sobrino, "The Witness of the Church in Latin America" in *The Challenge of Basic Christian Communities: Papers from the International Ecumenical Congress of Theology, February 20-March 2, 1980, Sao Paulo, Brazil*, eds. Sergio Torres and John Eagleson, trans. John Drury (Maryknoll: Orbis Books, 1981), p. 164. Cited hereafter as "Witness."

139Sobrino, *Jesus*, pp. 102-03.   140Sobrino, "Witness," pp. 163-69.

141For a more detailed analysis of this subject in relation to Christian spirituality, see Sobrino, *Spirituality*, pp. 87-102. Moltmann concurs with this idea. See Jürgen Moltmann, "Theology of Mystical Experience," *Scottish Journal of Theology*, 32 (1979), 513: "If we ask for the real underlying experience, the '*Sitz im Leben*,' of [discipleship], we come not on the religious but on the political, not on the monk but on the *martyr*."

142Sobrino, "Witness," pp. 170-74. For a detailed analysis of this type of persecution, see Sobrino, *True Church*, pp. 228-52.

143Jon Sobrino and Juan Hernández Pico, *Theology of Christian Solidarity*, trans. Phillip Berryman (Maryknoll: Orbis Books, 1985), pp. 15-25. For an example of this type of solidarity, see Sobrino, *Spirituality*, pp. 153-56.

144Jon Sobrino, "Current Problems in Christology in Latin American Theology," trans. Fernando Segovia in *Theology and Discovery: Essays in Honor of Karl Rahner, S.J.*, ed. William J. Kelly (Milwaukee, Wisconsin: Marquette University Press, 1980), pp. 199-201. Therefore, the church of the poor is an essential reason that Sobrino's doctrine of God has the content that it has: it reflects the experience of God in the church of the poor.

145Sobrino, *Christology*, p. 113.   146Sobrino, *Jesus*, p. 155.

147Sobrino, *Christology*, pp. 106-07. See pp. 123-27, where Sobrino proposed six "fundamental principles" that were necessary for a full understanding of discipleship. The first was "*the situation itself.*" Within a situation of injustice, one must find a place to stand in order to begin one's embodiment of justice. That place is with the poor. The second principle was "*the element of conflict.*" Conflict does not come about by the mere verbal proclamation of justice. It emerges full force when one actively struggles against injustice. The next principle was "*the 'conversion' of the subject.*" This process involves both a fundamental change in one's values and a giving up of oneself in service to God's kingdom. The "*absolute* character" of discipleship was the fourth principle. The eschatological nature of the kingdom puts people in a crisis. They must choose between two mutually exclusive alternatives: the status quo or the kingdom. The fifth principle was the "goal . . . of universal *reconciliation.*" This is accomplished by the doing of justice, understood as the re-creation of human beings and their world. Thus, justice embraces both individual reconciliation and social reconciliation. The final principle was "*openness to verification.*" True discipleship is verified objectively by the presence of justice and humanization. These partial historical embodiments of the kingdom are necessary for two reasons. First, they keep discipleship from regressing into "pure intention." Second, they prepare the disciple for future embodiments (this sixth principle is from Sobrino, *Jesus*, p. 137).

Chapter 4

LATIN AMERICAN CONTRIBUTIONS TO CONTEMPORARY CHRISTOLOGY

The purpose of this chapter is to delineate the contributions that liberation Christology makes to contemporary Christology. First, the individual contributions of Boff and Sobrino will be noted; then, somewhat artificially, they will be combined to form one set of contributions. The chapter ends with a final concluding statement.

The Contributions of Leonardo Boff

The contributions that Boff makes to the study of Christology are largely a matter of interpretation. This assessment is based upon the writer's knowledge of the larger christological scene and his own theological heritage. Since the conclusion entails a personal analysis of Latin American Christology, and because these points have already been discussed at length, the contributions will be stated with a minimal amount of elaboration.

The major contribution Boff makes is his delineation of five characteristics for a Latin American Christology: 1) primacy of the anthropological element over the ecclesiastical; 2) primacy of the utopian element over the factual; 3) primacy of the critical element over the dogmatic; 4) primacy of the social element over the personal; 5) primacy of orthopraxis over orthodoxy. While these involve no major changes in the content of Christology, they do provide a new way to access that content. This new way is the religious, social, political, and economic history of the continent. Despite its ties to Europe and North America, Latin America has developed along its own path; therefore, it is natural that it would also develop a theology reflecting its own cultural milieu.

A major part of this milieu is the marginalization of a great portion of the Latin American population. To reach these people, various priests and bishops began to speak of a "preferential option for the poor." They "re-discovered" Jesus' connection with people in everyday life: with shepherds, farmers, and mothers, and the important role they played in life; therefore, these pastors began doing theology *with* the poor rather than teaching it to them; learning from them while teaching them.

Another major contribution is Boff's starting point in Christology; namely, with the man, Jesus of Nazareth. In other words, Jesus' humanity is what is most accessible to people; therefore, the incarnation of God as a human being is where christological reflection ends. This allows twentieth century believers to walk in first century sandals: Jesus is seen as a prophet, an intriguing person, a crucified Messiah, and finally as the risen Lord; therefore, Boff still strikes a balance between the classical Chalcedonian christological confession of Jesus as truly human and truly divine, even though he begins with Jesus' humanity.

A corollary to this perspective is that the human quest for meaning is grounded in the story of Jesus. In the attempt to emulate the praxis of Jesus the believer may find a reason for living and, if necessary, a reason for dying. That reason is simply a life lived out to the end in terms of a being-for-others, that is, a liberative lifestyle of service to other people and to the great Other, God.

Third, Christology includes the call to discipleship. Jesus first said, "Come, follow me"; then he said, "Believe in me". In other words, discipleship forms the foundation for the comportment of Jesus' disciples, who are to act as their teacher acted. Orthodox Christology is a later development. From a Latin American point of view, orthopraxis is a better guarantee of orthodoxy than orthodoxy is of orthopraxis.

Boff also makes a strong case for the fact that belief in Jesus Christ should not be reduced to other-worldliness. Jesus himself was involved in the everyday life of his culture; he accepted parts of it and denounced others, all in the name of God and God's kingdom; therefore, the events central to Christian faith, the crucifixion and resurrection, are not merely salvific, or spiritual, in nature. They are the result and crowning glory of a specific lifestyle, a lifestyle lived out in the light of God's coming kingdom.

Much has been written on the centrality of the kingdom in Jesus' preaching. Boff has sought not only to affirm this, but also to ground Jesus' whole being in relation to it. His miracles are signs of the kingdom. His ministry is an incarnation of it. The call to discipleship is an invitation to live out kingdom values in the world. Therefore, the kingdom is to be preached, anticipated, and lived.

Boff's analysis of Jesus' death has three parts. First, he describes the crucifixion of Jesus as a crime. Jesus did nothing to deserve death; he was the innocent victim of a judicial system that was abused by the religious and political leaders of his day. Even though Jesus did not actively seek death, he integrated it into his faith, always trusting in the God whom he called "Abba." Second, Boff uncovers the contextuality of the interpretations of the crucifixion both in the New Testament and in the history of theology. This allows him to develop a new model for understanding Jesus' death: namely, as liberation. In doing so, Boff distances himself from Moltmann's model of the crucified God; Boff will have nothing to do with a crucifying God. Finally, Boff concludes that Jesus' death on the cross is a paradigm of meaningful suffering, that is, of completely giving one's life for the liberation of the oppressed which is also service to the kingdom of God.

In his writing about the work of the cosmic Christ, Boff has broadened the horizon of Christ's influence. Not only is he to be found working in the church and in individual Christians, Christ is also at work throughout the cosmos.

Wherever love, justice, equality, and mercy, that is, kingdom values, are found, one may find Christ at work continuing the ministry of Jesus of Nazareth.

Boff's Christology renews in his readers the original meaning of *euangelion*, namely, good news, hope, and life. While it is true to some extent that the gospel is bad news before it is good news, conservative theology has often over emphasized the bad news and relegated the good news to a spiritual plane. Boff does not deny the pervasiveness of sin; but his emphasis is upon liberation through God's grace, upon doing and acting rather than in refraining from acting.

A final contribution is Boff's reclamation of the birth narratives, which were one of the first casualties in the war between the scientific methodology of historical criticism and propositional theology. To a scientific mindset, facts were verifiable as true or false. Angels, the virgin birth, and the star, were viewed as false because they were unverifiable. Since Boff has placed these events at the end of the christological process, at the end of the early church's theological reflection upon the person and work of Jesus Christ, he has provided a way to reclaim them. The truth in these passages lies not in their verifiable facticity, detailed or otherwise, but in the fullness of their symbolism: this baby is God in the flesh, the liberator of all reality from the rule of sin.

The Contributions of Jon Sobrino

Sobrino has much to offer to the study of Christology. With Boff, he affirms the primacy of the historical Jesus. Sobrino avoids a literal, non-critical reading of the Gospels by his recognition of the insights of recent New Testament scholarship. Yet, he reads the Gospels with the eyes of faith; even though they are not biographies of Jesus, they are still credible witnesses to who Jesus was and what he did.

Sobrino agrees with Boff that the humanity of Jesus is the primary point of contact between human beings and Jesus. Sobrino's contribution here is that Jesus defines what it means to be human rather than being fitted into an abstract, *a priori* definition of humanity. A human being is both an individual and a social being: people relate one-to-one, one-to-group, and group-to-group. Human being is also vertical and horizontal being: people relate to God and to one another. How these different ways of relating are to be actualized is based upon Jesus as the prototype of being human. He is the prototype rather than the archetype because the former is dynamic in nature while the latter is static.

A corollary to this is Sobrino's contention that Jesus' whole life is a revelation. It cannot be cut into pieces and still have the same meaning. This is a corrective to the traditional emphasis upon Jesus' death and resurrection as *the* revelation of God. This two-sided event is meaningless, or at least ahistorical, if it is separated from the life that preceded it. This implies that the way one lives one's life is proof of one's acceptance of "Jesus as Lord and Savior."

Sobrino's interpretation of Jesus' death is both similar and dissimilar to that of Boff. Both contend that Jesus' death is a continuation of his life's mission to inaugurate God's kingdom; both highlight the religious and political dimensions of the crucifixion; and both emphasize the fact that discipleship often leads to death for the disciple. Sobrino's interpretation significantly differs from Boff's at several points. First, the crucifixion allows humanity to participate in, without exhausting the mystery of, the eternal life of God. Second, the crucifixion means that suffering and death are experiences common to both humanity and God. Third, Jesus' death questions the way humanity perceives God's revelation in the world. Finally, Sobrino describes Jesus' death as a scandal vis-à-vis God's abandonment of Jesus on the cross. Even though Sobrino echoes Moltmann at this point, he uses "scandal" in a different way. For him, the scandal resides in God's passivity on the cross, in God's permitting Jesus to die, and not in God's actively sending Jesus to die.

The distinction between doxological statements and historical statements is another contribution Sobrino makes. Too often faith is defined as belief in spite of the evidence; but if the traditional understanding of "faith in Jesus" as a call to discipleship is true, then this world and its history are important. Therefore, doxological statements, such as "God is love" and "Jesus is the Son of God," must be lived out and made credible within history. The basis of the way that is done today is none other than an orthopraxis which emulates the history of Jesus presented in the Gospels.

Directly related to this is Sobrino's emphasis upon discipleship or praxis as following Jesus, which is based upon the fact that, strictly speaking, Jesus reveals the Son. This does not negate the fact that Jesus also reveals the "fullness of the Godhead." It means that his revelation of God is indirect through his proclamation of God's kingdom and his fidelity to God. In his revelation as the Son, Jesus concretized the process of filiation, that is, the way in which one becomes a child of God. This process not only involves the traditional belief in Jesus; it involves also living life as he lived it by offering oneself in service to God's kingdom. Sobrino is not ingenuous; he knows the "cost of discipleship." Situating God's love in a sinful world results in crucifixion of some sort; but if one wishes to be a Christian, a child of God, there is no other way.

Sobrino's dynamic understanding of God's kingdom is another contribution. He goes beyond stating that Jesus proclaimed the kingdom of God. For Sobrino, God is acting in history in order to transform it into a community of brothers and sisters. The essence of the kingdom is grace: it is based upon God's initiative for the betterment of humankind. This dynamic view also broadens the concept of sin to include both the vertical and horizontal natures of human being. If one sins against God, one sins against people. Likewise, if one sins against another person, one also sins against God.

This leads to another contribution Sobrino makes in his Christology: Jesus defines what divinity is rather than being defined by an abstract, *a priori* conception of divinity. For Sobrino, this means that the God of Jesus is a God of life. This view calls for a reformulation of the traditional attributes of God in terms of love and grace rather than in terms of power and honor. It means also that Jesus' suffering and death must be seen as essential to God's nature. For the belief that

"God is love" to be credible to humanity, God's love must be situated in a world pervaded by sin. The cross reveals the final consequence of this action. God's power in the resurrection inspires the hope that justice ultimately will triumph over injustice; that God's definitive kingdom will, indeed, be a community of brothers and sisters.

Sobrino's greatest contribution is found in his five hermeneutical guideposts: 1) the theological milieu of the author; 2) the author's attitude toward the Enlightenment; 3) the kind of hermeneutics employed by an author; 4) the way the fundamental metaphysical quandary is posed; and 5) the density of an author's christological concentration. These points allow him to do two things. First, he is able to state his christological presuppositions, which enables him to dialogue with other contemporary Christologies and with the church's christological dogmas. This dialogue is negative in that Sobrino argues against what he perceives to be non-liberative elements in them. It is positive in that he constructs a Christology relevant to Latin America based on elements already extant in traditional Roman Catholic Christology. Second, he places himself within the broader context of theology and history. Even though he is writing as a Latin American to Latin Americans, he cannot ignore the philosophical and theological movements that impact Europe, since Latin America was colonized by Europeans and still draws much of its religious and cultural identity from Europe.

LATIN AMERICAN CONTRIBUTIONS TO CONTEMPORARY CHRISTOLOGY

The final section of this chapter is an attempt to combine the individual contributions of Boff and Sobrino into one set. To this writer, liberation Christology offers three major contributions, namely, 1) the recognition of contextuality; 2) a Latin American version of Christology "from below"; and 3) the theological import of liberation Christology.

Recognition of Contextuality

Latin American liberation Christology is first and foremost a Christology for Latin America. It is a response to the Latin American experience of colonialism and social, political, and economic oppression. This response is summed up in the word "liberation" and the title, "the Liberator," to designate Jesus Christ. The explicit recognition of the Latin American situation calls for an equally explicit recognition of christological presuppositions. The best statement of liberation Christology's presuppositions is found in Sobrino's five hermeneutical guideposts: 1) the theological milieu of the author; 2) the author's attitude toward the Enlightenment; 3) the kind of hermeneutics employed by an author; 4) the way the fundamental metaphysical quandary is posed; and 5) the density of an author's christological concentration.

When these five guideposts are employed, they will follow the tenor of Boff's five guidelines: 1) primacy of the anthropological element over the ecclesiastical; 2) primacy of the utopian element over the factual; 3) primacy of the critical element over the dogmatic; 4) primacy of the social element over the personal; and 5) the primacy of orthopraxis over orthodoxy. For this writer, Boff's guidelines complement those of Sobrino; for example, oppression, as an author's milieu, is primarily a social phenomenon; therefore, communal experiences of oppression are emphasized over personal ones. This is not to overlook the personal element because individuals also experience oppression. The intent is to prioritize these two experiences. In Latin America today, oppression has become institutionalized; it has a life of its own; thus, the social aspect of oppression precedes that of the individual.

A corollary to this aspect of contextuality also concerns non-Latin American Christologies. They, too, are situation specific. To a limited degree, this was implicitly stated; for example, Wolfhart Pannenberg analyzes the christological writings of the nineteenth century, which allows him to present the continuity and discontinuity of his Christology with earlier ones. The same is true of his interaction with the post-Bultmannians.[1] The difference between Pannenberg and liberation Christology is that Pannenberg does not state for whom his Christology is intended, while liberation Christology does.

The same criticism may be directed to Jürgen Moltmann, who begins his discussion of "the crucified God" from the generic standpoints of the "Christian life" and "Christian faith."[2] This presupposes a common understanding of these terms for everyone. Moltmann then proceeds to discuss "the resistance of the cross against its interpretations."[3] His examples are almost exclusively European. The exceptions are those of Kazoh Kitamori and James H. Cone. Like Pannenberg, Moltmann writes primarily for Europeans and secondarily for a wider audience; however, he does not state this explicitly.[4]

It follows from this that Christology must be relevant to a specific historical situation before it can be applied to other situations. In other words, liberation Christology must speak first to the Latin American experience of colonialism and oppression. Only then can it enter into dialogue with other contemporary Christologies. To be sure, Pannenberg and Moltmann have done this implicitly. The contribution of liberation Christology is the challenge to do so explicitly. Relevance to a specific situation has two results. First, Christology will be grounded historically according to the needs and aspirations of a specific group of people. Second, relevance to a particular people and time calls for an inductive approach to Christology, which is to say, the universal significance of Jesus Christ depends upon his significance to a particular people.

The second aspect of contextuality evident in liberation Christology is its foundation in "the other side of history," that is, in the poor and oppressed. This is represented in liberation Christology's "preferential option for the poor"; its critique of systemic evil and oppression; and its use of the term, "liberation," rather than the traditional "salvation." Pannenberg has not really addressed the problems of the poor and oppressed.[5] Moltmann does make more summary and systematic references to the privileged position of the poor and oppressed vis-à-vis God's kingdom. The positive aspect of "the Mysticism of the Cross" is the identification of the downtrodden and suffering with the "poor, suffering, unprotected Christ." If such a Christ was resurrected, then the oppressed may hope in God's future restoration of their full humanity.[6]

The critique of systemic evil and oppression is paramount in liberation Christology, but they are not primary in Pannenberg's Christology. To the extent that he does deal with them, he seems sympathetic to liberation Christology. First, he makes the point that a community deriving from the Old Testament will participate in the socio-political world. Pannenberg does not see this as an essential break with Jesus because "public responsibility . . . did not confront" him in the way it does Christians today. This is probably due to Jesus' "imminent eschatological expectation"; but "changed historical conditions" lead to active political involvement for later generations.[7]

Unfortunately, Pannenberg gives little indication as to the form political involvement might take, in spite of the fact that, in the mid-1960s, he "became considerably less optimistic" about the "moral superiority [and] historical future of the values of the liberal democratic tradition."[8] One reason for this is his rejection of Marxism as a viable option for Christian political action. Pannenberg argues that Christianity and Marxism are incompatible for three reasons: 1) Marxism is unapologetically atheistic; which results in 2) an anthropology that replaces God with a humanity defined solely in socio-economic terms; and 3) the dismal history of communism in Russia and Eastern Europe.[9]

Another reason for this deficiency is an underdeveloped "criteria of justice" in Pannenberg's theology, which is surprising since he has:

> stressed the necessity for criteria of justice that flow from a Christian theory of social justice and was highly critical of liberation theologians . . .for having "no interest" in such criteria.[10]

Pannenberg has done little to remedy this situation. Even though he is critical of the "simplistic" treatment of exploitation and justice at the hands of Marxism and liberation theology, he still laments the absence of a "generally acceptable concept of justice."[11]

Second, Pannenberg speaks of sin in terms of one's "relation to things and men. . . . as a consequence of their behavior."[12] This is, in part, due to Pannenberg's criticism of Marxist humanism, that is, its "reduction of the individual to a function of social interaction."[13] Such a reduction not only disregards "individual human rights" and deprives the individual of "autonomy and human dignity," it also contradicts the basic Christian belief "that human beings are creatures of God."[14] Still his emphasis is upon individual rather than corporate sin.[15]

Moltmann is more specific: Jesus proclaimed the kingdom of God to the victims of systemic oppression. He himself was a victim of systemic evil. He identified with "the human way of life and practice chosen by . . . weak, lowly and despised persons" who, through their powerlessness, protested against their oppression by their faith in God's coming kingdom.[16]

According to Latin American Christology, the content of Jesus' life and message is summed up in the word, "liberation." To be sure, traditional terms, such as "salvation" and "redemption," do occur; but only in the context of liberation. Pannenberg, however, does not utilize this term often, if at all. This is due to the nature of *Jesus--God and Man*: it is primarily an academic endeavor. As such, Pannenberg dialogues with the major trends and figures in the history of Christology. This should not be interpreted as a fault on Pannenberg's part because liberation, in the religio-political sense of the word today, was not an issue in the early sixties in Germany. On the other hand, Pannenberg's emphasis on the history of Jesus, "revelation as history," and the futurity of God could be altered and adapted into the basic building blocks for founding a viable liberation Christology.[17]

Moltmann's affinity for "liberation" is both implicit and explicit. It is implicit in what he says concerning the poor and oppressed, and in his criticism of structural sin. It is explicit in his discussion of psychological and political liberation.[18] Moltmann examines the former before the latter, which implies the primacy of the personal element over the social. In his discussion of psychological liberation, Moltmann does not differentiate between the psychological, emotional, and physical needs of the poor and those of more affluent people. In other words, he remains on the level of generalities, of the way theology may appropriate psychoanalytical thought. His discussion of political liberation is more specific: He names oppressive structures: capitalism, technocracy, and racism.[19] He advocates liberative actions: socialism, democracy, ecology, and wholeness.[20] In all of this, he does not begin with the oppressed, but from a position of power he issues the challenge to take a stand with the victims of oppression. To be sure, this is a necessary step for the socio-political liberation of all; but it is not the same as being oppressed and calling for liberation. Moltmann does not make this difference clear.

The third aspect of contextuality is the necessity for theological dialogue. No one theologian, or geographical collection of theologians, can see the totality of reality. There is a need for a "fusion of horizons," as Hans-Georg Gadamer says. The impact of Pannenberg and Moltmann upon liberation Christology is evidence of this dialogue. Even though they are not poor and oppressed, they still have something to offer to the poor. In the same vein, Moltmann acknowledges the influence of liberation theology upon his understanding of political liberation.[21] Practically speaking, partial embodiments of God's kingdom are impossible if the oppressed and their affluent advocates do not work together. This does not mean that both groups must use the same hermeneutic, methodology, concepts, or words; but they do need a common goal and a common understanding of that goal. Once this process of commonality is underway, the oppressed may move toward the goal in their own unique way while their advocates move in theirs. Thus, both groups will be faithful to their own concrete situation, to each other, and to the kingdom of God.

Christology "from Below"

The second major contribution of liberation Christology to contemporary Christology is its version of a Christology "from below." The uniqueness of this version is evident in five areas: 1) its emphasis upon the humanity of Jesus; 2) Jesus' proclamation of the kingdom of God; 3) Jesus' call to discipleship as a part of Christology; 4) the work of the cosmic Christ; and 5) the reclamation of the birth narratives. Liberation Christology's emphasis upon Jesus' humanity is seen in its contention that the starting point of Christology is the historical Jesus. Thus, the correct method for understanding Jesus Christ is chronological, to follow the historical course of the disciples' encounter with the man Jesus to the church's confession of him as Lord.

To be sure, the historical Jesus plays an important role for both Pannenberg and Moltmann; but it is not the same role as in liberation Christology. Pannenberg asserts that "Christology must begin with the man Jesus [but] its first question has to be that about his unity with God."[22]   In other words, his Christology "from below" begins with the historical Jesus by first establishing his divinity; however, logical consistency favors the tack of liberation Christology: starting with the historical Jesus means beginning with his humanity and showing the way his divinity is revealed in and through his life, death, and resurrection.

Moltmann, too, stresses the place of the historical Jesus in Christology.[23] Even so, when he discusses the "questions about Jesus," the first question he addresses is, "Is Jesus true God?"; then he turns to the question of Jesus' humanity.[24] Moltmann's methodology implies that the divinity of Jesus is the crucial issue for Christology and that the cross of Jesus, because it is an intra-trinitarian event, is the primary stumbling-block to faith in God. Therefore, Pannenberg and Moltmann presuppose the humanity of Jesus while substantiating his divinity, whereas liberation finds it necessary to verify both his humanity and divinity in that order.

Based upon this methodology, liberation Christology contends that Jesus' whole life is revelatory, not just his cross and resurrection; which is to say, Jesus' death and resurrection are meaningless if separated from his life. For Pannenberg, Jesus' life and message find meaning in his resurrection from the dead, which is consistent with Pannenberg's emphasis on the proleptic nature of the resurrection.[25] It is also reflected in his "substantiation" of "Jesus' personal unity with God" via the resurrection prior to his explication of Jesus' humanity. Unfortunately, this also opens the door for the absorption of Jesus' humanity by his divinity.

Moltmann, on the other hand, virtually reduces Jesus' revelation of God to the crucifixion. He plainly states: "Christian faith stands and falls with the knowledge of the crucified Christ, that is, with the knowledge of God *in* the crucified Christ."[26] Moltmann does not ignore the history of Jesus' proclamation of God's kingdom to the poor; but this revelation pales in comparison to the revelation of God on the cross, for the cross is an intra-trinitarian event.[27] Moltmann, like Pannenberg, stresses Jesus' divinity over his humanity. Liberation Christology, however, argues that Jesus' divinity has no meaning outside its concretization in his life as a human being.

Liberation Christology agrees with Pannenberg and Moltmann that Jesus' death resulted from his life, specifically, as a consequence of his proclamation of

God's kingdom. This implies three things. First, Jesus died for a religious reason: blasphemy. Pannenberg contends that blasphemy, "Jesus' claim of an authority properly belonging only to God," was the real reason the Jewish authorities took action against Jesus.[28]   For Moltmann, Jesus died a blasphemer because he contradicted the understanding of the Law held by the religious power brokers: the kingdom of God is for the poor, oppressed, sinners, and tax collectors.[29]

Second, Jesus was crucified as a rebel against the Roman Empire. According to Moltmann, Jesus died thusly because the liberation inherent in his proclamation of God's kingdom was a "challenge to the *Pax Romana* and its gods and laws."[30]   Pannenberg, however, is not convinced of this aspect of Jesus' death. To be sure, Jesus was crucified by Roman authority; but this participation was "conditioned by slanderous accusations, and not motivated by the essence of Jesus' claim."[31]   At best, Pannenberg says that "Jesus' activity" was more revolutionary than that of any revolutionary because "his eschatological message took away the glitter of ultimacy from every human political order."[32]

Third, Jesus did not actively seek his death. Pannenberg argues that "Jesus' fate" was not "actively accomplished" by him.[33]   Moltmann, too, argues that Jesus' crucifixion was "the consequence of his ministry and as the consequence of the reactions of the Jews and the Romans to his ministry."[34]   The difference between Pannenberg and Moltmann and liberation Christology is the latter's explicit contention that Jesus proclaimed the good news of the kingdom of God to the poor as a poor man. Such a total identification with the poor was bound to bring him into conflict with the religious and political systems of his day. That he was put to death shows how thoroughly these systems understood his message of liberation.

Another contribution is Latin American Christology's contention that in his history Jesus revealed the Son of God and the way the Son relates to the Father. Only indirectly, within this history, does Jesus reveal the Father. The implication of this is that anyone who would be a child of God must also act in this manner. Pannenberg's view of the content of Jesus' revelation is both similar and dissimilar to that of liberation Christology. The similarity resides in his contention that the distinction between Jesus of Nazareth and God reflects the distinction between the eternal Son and the Father.[35]   Dissimilarity is seen in God's "revelational presence" in Jesus. Here Pannenberg is one with contemporary theology that revelation equals self-revelation: "the Revealer and what is revealed are identical."[36]

Moltmann also holds to this definition of revelation. For him, Jesus' life, culminating in the crucifixion, is an unveiling of the true nature of God. This is seen in two ways. First, Moltmann does not interact with any christological dogmas, implying his presupposition of them. Second, from the beginning to the end of *The Crucified God*, he speaks of the Son's relationship to the Father, which implies his presupposition of Jesus' divinity.[37]

If Jesus reveals the way to become a child of God, it follows that human meaningfulness is grounded in the story of Jesus. For liberation Christology, a meaningful life is summarized by the word "pro-existence." This word means living one's life for others, both other people and God. Pannenberg emphasizes the latter. Openness to the world is future oriented, toward humanity's ultimate destiny; namely, resurrection.[38] Therefore, openness to the world is fulfilled by openness to God and God's future.[39] This living for God comes before living for others. Liberation Christology agrees that openness to God is ultimate, but asserts that it is meaningless without openness to the world; living for God and for others is a simultaneous rather than a chronological activity.

Moltmann is closer to the liberation perspective. In his discussion of the *"vicious circles of death,"* the circles of poverty, force, racial and cultural alienation, and ecological destruction are examined before the circle of "senselessness and godforsakenness," implying that all five circles must be eradicated.[40] This view is corroborated by his belief that these circles of death are overcome by a "liberation [characterized by] a significant life filled with the sense of the whole."[41] Moltmann's shortcoming is that he offers no indications as to the way affluent Christians are to attempt such a liberation from a general position of advocacy for the poor and oppressed.

The second aspect of a liberation Christology "from below" is its presentation of Jesus' relationship to the kingdom of God. In this view, the kingdom is the determining factor of Jesus' life and praxis. Indirectly, it is the God of the kingdom, which reflects the contention of liberation Christology that God's being is known only through God's liberative acts in history. Therefore, Jesus' praxis of healing and forgiving sins (his proclamation of God's kingdom by deeds) indirectly reveal the God of the kingdom to be a God of life who liberates humanity because of God's love for humanity. This is in contrast to both Pannenberg and Moltmann, who have the Father as the primary reference point in Jesus' life.[42]

Liberation Christology's view of Jesus' relationship to the kingdom broadens the concept of sin to include the social dimension of human sin along with the personal. The former is given priority because of the corporate nature of poverty and oppression as experienced in Latin America. Pannenberg stresses the personal, individual aspect of sin, but this does not mean he ignores corporate sin.[43] His discussion of the scapegoat implies a recognition of this phenomenon.[44] He also notes that some individuals are affected by corporate sin more than others; but these two references are the exception rather than the rule in his discussion of sin.[45]

Because Moltmann is more liberation oriented, social sin plays more of a role for him, which is evidenced in his use of "the poor," "the oppressed," and "the downtrodden."[46] It is also evident in his discussion of the "vicious circles of death."[47] But his recognition of the social nature of sin is not usually seen in conjunction with Jesus' proclamation of God's kingdom.

Another aspect of Jesus' proclamation of the kingdom that liberation Christology highlights is its dynamic nature. God's kingdom is not merely a concept Jesus chose to accentuate; rather, it is a life-changing force that transforms individuals and society. Since it is *God's* kingdom, it is experienced as grace, which was hinted at above when it was said that God's being is revealed by God's liberative acts in history. Pannenberg sounds close to this view: the nearness of the kingdom relativizes all human social and political orders.[48] He also contends that Jesus' "commandment to love," including one's enemies, is the criterion for kingdom comportment.[49] Still, he does not get beyond general statements as to the way the kingdom may change individuals and societies today.

Moltmann comes much closer. For him, God's kingdom comes as grace rather than judgment. This gracious act of God is:

> anticipated by the word of the gospel which Jesus preached and his living offering of himself to the poor, the sinners and the tax collectors . . . by which the lost are sought out and those without rights, and the unrighteous, are accepted.[50]

Moltmann offers little definite direction for embodying this grace today apart from his general discussion of the "ways toward the political liberation of man."

Thus, God's kingdom is essential to liberation Christology's understanding of human liberation. While the kingdom is important to Pannenberg, its role and importance is more explicit in Moltmann and Latin American Christology. Ultimately, the kingdom is liberation for humankind and all creation. Penultimately, or historically, the kingdom is in process. Wherever there is the striving for freedom for others and God, wherever women and men are enabled to love one another more fully, one can see a partial embodiment of God's eschatological kingdom.

The third aspect of a liberation Christology "from below" is its contention that Christology is the foundation of discipleship. Thus, liberation Christology interprets Jesus' praxis as a counterbalance to other-worldliness and as a lifestyle that leads to crucifixion. As has been the case so far, Pannenberg speaks of following Jesus in true but general statements. He argues that "if faith determines the entire life of the Christian, then it is important that it be, even in its structure, discipleship, participation in Jesus' way, in his behavior."[51] Following "in Jesus' way" results in "the eschatological community of justice," and includes "love for the enemy."[52] The kingdom of God determines how the eschatological community participates in the political realm. For Pannenberg, God's kingdom is the "fulfillment of justice among men."[53] Therefore, partial embodiments of the kingdom are recognizable by the presence, and increase, of justice in the world. Apart from his rejection of Marxism as a viable option, Pannenberg does not project possible courses of action for concretizing this love, who the enemy might be, or the cost of loving and forgiving the enemy.

Moltmann is more specific: "Christian theology," and by implication, Christians and the church, must take sides vis-à-vis oppression. The disciples of Jesus cannot be sensitive to the cries of the oppressed and "always be on the side of the rulers of this world. [They] must come to terms with the cry of the wretched for God and for freedom out of the depths of the sufferings of this age."[54] Having said this, Moltmann does not feel compelled to give his readers any hints on the way to stand with "the wretched," or when it is appropriate to do so, or the criteria by which to measure "the rulers of this world."

The frightening part of discipleship in liberation Christology is its contention that following Jesus may lead to crucifixion. In relation to oppression, one is either part of the problem or part of the solution. Being an active part of the solution in Latin America may lead to arrest, torture, and often, death. In this context, death is not merely an individual experience; it also affects the economic and social life of the deceased's family and community.

Pannenberg acknowledges this precarious position of Jesus' disciples today. He writes: "life under the Lordship of Christ in this world repeatedly leads Christians to a participation in the cross of Jesus."[55] The cross is the consequence of the Christian's task to announce the coming kingdom of God just as it was for Jesus. Based upon the context of this statement, Pannenberg seems to say that announcing the kingdom is equivalent to actualizing it in history. Once again, Pannenberg does not attempt to give any specific guidance to his readers. Does "participation in the cross of Jesus" entail literal death? Or is he referring to some type of social, economic, or political sacrifice on the part of the individual or community? Or, are both understandings possible depending on the situation? Pannenberg does not say.

The cross plays a part in discipleship for Moltmann, also. Following Jesus means accepting "not only suffering and a bitter fate, but the suffering of rejection."[56] Thus, the cross of the disciple is defined by the cross of Jesus; it results from obedience to the mission of proclaiming the kingdom of God, which evokes conflict and death. But the disciple does not die godforsaken as Jesus did; rather, the disciple dies "in fellowship with [Jesus]."[57] In speaking this way, Moltmann almost includes crucifixion as an integral part of discipleship. Even so, he does not say whether or not it is a literal or figurative death.

The fourth aspect of a liberation Christology "from below" is the work of the cosmic Christ. The risen Lord is the same one who was crucified; therefore, the work of the cosmic Christ is the same as that of Jesus of Nazareth: the actualization of God's kingdom in the world. It follows from this that wherever women and men strive for justice and liberation from all forms of oppression, the cosmic Christ is at work. This does not minimize the place of Christians or the church in the proclamation of God's kingdom; rather, it allows the church to find allies it did not know it had. Pannenberg advocates a similar view. For him, the church is relativized because it "anticipates the coming reality of the Kingdom of God."[58] Even though it embodies the destiny of all humanity, it is still a "provisional" form of the kingdom. Its task is to call "the whole world into the obedience of sonship to the Father and his coming Kingdom."[59] Pannenberg does not say whether or not non-Christians have a part in the kingdom. Nor does he entertain the possibility that non-Christian religions are situation-specific responses to the working of the cosmic Christ.[60]

The final aspect of a liberation Christology "from below" is its reclamation of the birth narratives of Jesus. It is well known that these passages have fallen on hard times in contemporary theology. The virgin birth is classified as mythological in the sense of "speaking of the divine" and as "untrue." The timing of the star and the adoration of the shepherds and Magi are difficult to ascertain and coalesce. But if the birth narratives are seen as theological statements, as symbols, as myth in the sense of speaking of the divine, their facticity is not so great an issue. In other words, the truth of the birth narratives--that the baby in the manger is the son of God, the Savior of the world, and is worthy of worship by all people regardless of rank--is not dependent upon their having happened in exactly the way presented by Matthew and Luke. Thus, one does not have to read and interpret these passages literally in order to understand their meaning. Nor does a non-literal reading prohibit one's appreciation of them in their present form. Pannenberg discusses only one aspect of the birth narratives: the virgin birth. One may assume that he would treat other problematic parts in the same way. According to him, the significance of the virgin birth lies in "its concern that Jesus was God's Son from the beginning, that he is therefore the Son of God in person."[61] He contends that the "theologoumenon" of the virgin birth has a place in the "liturgical confession of the church" because of its "antidocetic and antiadoptionistic" point of view.[62] Apart from this function, it has no theological value.[63]

Theological Significance of
Liberation Christology

The theological significance of liberation Christology is primarily methodological in nature. First, it contends that Christology is the starting point for theology, that is, divine nature, human nature, salvation, sin, and eschatology cannot be understood properly apart from the history of Jesus.[64] The following serves as an indication of what it means to have a christological interpretation of theology. Jesus' proclamation of the kingdom of God reveals the true nature of God: God is a God of life who desires liberation for humanity and creation. Jesus' praxis in obedience to this mission unveils the true nature of human beings: they exist for others and for God. Eschatology is defined primarily in terms of "ultimate things" rather than "final things"; history is fulfilled by the final establishment of God's kingdom. Salvation is liberation from all forms of oppression that prohibit individuals and societies from living for others and God. Sin is an attitude that results in actions that work against the actualization of the kingdom in the world. The church is the community of people who have consciously accepted the responsibility to continue the mission of Jesus: to announce the coming of God's kingdom and to actualize it, as much as is humanly possible, in the world. The Christian life is nothing less than following Jesus, embodying the same praxis he did in relation to the poor and oppressed and oppressive structures.

Second, Jesus reveals God, and God's will for humanity, indirectly; God cannot be known directly by human beings. God's presence in the world is mediated through historical events, which protects the ultimate mystery of God; it lets God be God. This mediation is also the means by which individuals live a meaningful life. Every human attitude and action has the possibility of mediating God to the world; every situation in which people find themselves has the possibility of revealing new things about God. These possibilities depend upon whether or not individuals and societies are striving for the liberation inherent in Jesus' proclamation of God's kingdom. Insofar as they are liberation oriented, they indirectly reveal God to the world.

The third impact is the relationship between doxological statements and historical statements. The latter refer to the historical acts by which God reveals Godself. The former are statements about the essence of God based upon God's acts in history. The presupposition underlying this relationship is that doxological statements must be verifiable, which precludes two things. First, it prohibits any *a priori* knowledge of divine nature, human nature, salvation, sin, and so on. Second, it guards against manipulations of God that are based upon abstract conceptions of divinity.

The final impact is found in liberation Christology's emphasis upon the "goodness" of the gospel. It stresses "You shall" rather than "You shall not." Therefore, "You shall": love God with all your being and your neighbor as yourself; attempt to actualize God's kingdom in the world; care for the hungry, the needy, the poor and oppressed. To be sure, this entails conflict: One will experience the full power of sin as it is mediated by religious, political, and economic structures. Even so, one will be following the way of Jesus and verifying that one is a child of God.

Notes

[1]Wolfhart Pannenberg, *Jesus--God and Man*, 2nd ed. trans. Lewis L. Wilkins and Duane A. Priebe (Philadelphia: Westminster Press, 1968), pp. 22-30. Cited hereafter as *Jesus*.

[2]Jürgen Moltmann, *The Crucified God: The Cross of Christ as the Foundation and Criticism of Christian Theology*, trans. R. A. Wilson and John Bowden (New York: Harper & Row, 1974), pp. 8-24. Cited hereafter as *Crucified God*.

[3]Ibid., pp. 32-75.

[4]Moltmann has become more aware of this problem. See Jürgen Moltmann, *The Church in the Power of the Spirit: A Contribution to Messianic Ecclesiology*, trans. Margaret Kohl (New York: Harper and Row, 1977), pp. xiii-xvii, cited hereafter as *Church*; *The Trinity and the Kingdom: The Doctrine of God*, trans. Margaret Kohl (New York: Harper and Row, 1981), pp. xi-xvi, cited hereafter as *Trinity*; "The Inviting Unity of the Triune God," trans. Robert Nowell in *Monotheism*, eds. Claude Geffré and Jean-Pierre Jossua (Edinburgh: T and T Clark, 1985), pp. 50-51; *God in Creation: A New Theology of Creation and the Spirit of God: The Gifford Lectures 1984-1985*, trans. Margaret Kohl (New York: Harper and Row, 1985), pp. xi-xv; and "Christian Theology and Political Religion," in *Civil Religion and Political Theology*, ed. Leroy S. Rouner (Notre Dame: University of Notre Dame Press, 1986), pp. 41-45. See also Wolfhart Pannenberg, *Anthropology in Theological Perspective*, trans. Matthew J. O'Connell (Philadelphia: Westminster, 1985), pp. 11-23, cited hereafter as *Anthropology*.

[5]For example, Wolfhart Pannenberg, "A Theology of the Cross," *Word and World*, VIII (1988), 167 and "The Resurrection of Jesus and the Future of Mankind," trans. M. B. Jackson in *The Cumberland Seminarian*, XIX (1981), 44-45. He addressed this subject only exegetically in *Jesus*.

6Moltmann, *Crucified God*, pp. 47-53. See also pp. 127-28: Jesus' living for God and his proclamation of "the gospel of the kingdom for the poor" provoke the religious and political power structures to crucify him. Cf. Moltmann, *Church*, pp. 78-80.

7Pannenberg, *Jesus*, pp. 237-40.

8Wolfhart Pannenberg, "God's Presence in History," *The Christian Century*, March 11, 1981, p. 263.

9Wolfhart Pannenberg, "Christianity, Marxism, and Liberation Theology," *Christian Scholars Review*, 18 (1989), 215-21, cited hereafter as "Christianity." See also Gary M. Simpson summary of Pannenberg's critique of Marxism in "Whither Wolfhart Pannenberg? Reciprocity and Political Theology," *The Journal of Religion*, 67 (1987), 37-38, cited hereafter as "Whither Pannenberg." Thus, Pannenberg rejects liberation theology because of its erroneous belief that Marxist analysis can be used without a wholesale acceptance of Marxist ideology and its use of the concept, "neo-colonialism," which originated in Lenin's apology for some of the basic failures of Marxist theory (ibid., 224-25).

10Simpson, "Whither Pannenberg," 43.

11Pannenberg, "Christianity," 222 and 226. See also Wolfhart Pannenberg, *Christian Spirituality* (Philadelphia: Westminster Press, 1983), pp. 50-70: "Sanctification and Politics."

12Pannenberg, *Jesus*, p. 353. Cf. Wolfhart Pannenberg, *Theology and the Kingdom of God*, trans. Richard John Neuhaus (Philadelphia: Westminster Press, 1969), pp. 122-24: Pannenberg discussed the political implications of the relationship between the majority, minorities, and the commonweal in democratic societies. The point here is that the corporate reality of sin and oppression plays a minor role in his Christology. Cf. Pannenberg's discussion of the social aspect of human life in his book, *The Apostles' Creed in the Light of Today's Questions*, trans. Margaret Kohl (Philadelphia: Westminster, 1972), pp. 87-90. Cited hereafter as *Apostles' Creed*.

13Pannenberg, "Christianity," 217.   14Ibid., 217-18.

15Cf. Simpson, "Whither Pannenberg," 41, but also 48.

16Moltmann, *Crucified God*, p. 70. See also n. 6 above.

17While Pannenberg's influence on liberation theology is undeniable, his appreciation of that influence is another question. See Pannenberg, "Christianity," 217-25 for his criticism of Marxism and, by association, liberation theology. Simpson observed that Pannenberg's criticism was based on his observation of Marxism in Eastern Europe rather than the various socialist experiments in Latin America (Simpson, "Whither Pannenberg," 49).

18Moltmann, *Crucified God*, pp. 291-316: "Ways Toward the Psychological Liberation of Man" and pp. 317-40: "Ways Toward the Political Liberation of Man."

19Ibid., p. 320.   20Ibid., pp. 332-34.

[21]Ibid., pp. 287, n. 124 and 338, n. 1. See also Moltmann, *Church*, pp. 17-18; 364, n. 22; 394, n. 108; 400, n. 18; 401, n. 26; and Moltmann, *Trinity*, pp. 226, n. 5 and n. 9 and 252, n. 45.

[22]Pannenberg, *Jesus*, p. 36. See also p. 407: "The presentation of Jesus' deity, then, is not finished with *Part One* [The Knowledge of Jesus' Divinity], but forms the overarching theme of the entire book. In this perspective the function of working out the difference between Jesus and the Father becomes the main objective of the treatment of Jesus' humanity in *Part Two* [Jesus the Man Before God]."

[23]Moltmann, *Crucified God*, pp. 82-111.   [24]Ibid., pp. 87-98.

[25]Pannenberg, *Jesus*, pp. 66-73.   [26]Moltmann, *Crucified God*, p. 65.

[27]Ibid., pp. 200-78, esp. pp. 235-49.   [28]Pannenberg, *Jesus*, pp. 252-53.

[29]Moltmann, *Crucified God*, pp. 128-34.   [30]Ibid., pp. 143-44.

[31]Pannenberg, *Jesus*, p. 260.

[32]Ibid., p. 261. See also Pannenberg, *Apostles' Creed*, pp. 85-87. Pannenberg argued that Pilate, as the representative of Rome, "demonstrates the tendency of political rule to violate the majesty of God, a tendency which operates everywhere where political rule usurps absolute binding forces" (p. 86).

[33]Pannenberg, *Jesus*, p. 245. See also Pannenberg, *Apostles' Creed*, pp. 78-79.

[34]Moltmann, *Crucified God*, p. 128.   [35]Pannenberg, *Jesus*, pp. 158-60.

[36]Ibid., p. 129.

[37]See Moltmann, *Crucified God*, p. 149: the "origin of Christology" lies in what occurred between Jesus and his "Father" in his life, preaching, and abandonment on the cross; p. 151: the cry of dereliction expresses what is happening "between God and God"; and p. 243: the "Fatherlessness" of the Son is paralleled by the "Sonlessness" of God. Nowhere does Moltmann establish this "familial" relationship.

[38]Pannenberg, *Jesus*, pp. 85-88.   [39]Ibid., p. 226.

[40]Moltmann, *Crucified God*, pp. 330-32.   [41]Ibid., p. 334.

[42]See the discussion above, pp. 194-98, on the content of Jesus' revelation. That Jesus reveals God implies that Jesus' relationship to God has priority over his relationship to God's kingdom.

[43]For example, see Pannenberg, *Jesus*, pp. 364-65; p. 250; esp. p. 353: "Rather, *a man* falls into sin and thereby into contradiction against God through his relation to things and men. . . ." (emphasis added).

[44]Ibid., p. 265.   [45]Ibid., pp. 264-65.

46For example, Moltmann, *Crucified God*, pp. 45-53.   47Ibid., pp. 329-35.

48Pannenberg, *Jesus*, p. 239.

49Ibid., pp. 232-35, esp. p. 234: "To this extent, love does not contrast with justice, but is rather itself . . . the creation of new forms of justice appropriate to the respective situation."

50Moltmann, *Crucified God*, pp. 129-30. See also Jürgen Moltmann, "God's Kingdom as the Meaning of Life and of the World," trans. Theo Weston in *Why Did God Make Me?* eds. Hans Küng and Jürgen Moltmann (New York: Seabury Press, 1978), pp. 100-03.

51Pannenberg, *Jesus*, p. 199.   52Ibid., pp. 234-36.   53Ibid., p. 376.

54Moltmann, *Crucified God*, p. 153. Cf. Jürgen Moltmann, "Theology of Mystical Experience," *Scottish Journal of Theology*, 32 (1979), 514, where he argued that discipleship results in prison, torture, and death. He writes: "In prison the soul finds the *unio mystica*. That we can hear from the 'cloud of witnesses' in Korea, South Africa, Latin America, and other lands" (ibid.).

55Pannenberg, *Jesus*, p. 375.   56Moltmann, *Crucified God*, p. 55.   57Ibid., p. 56.

58Pannenberg, *Jesus*, p. 373.   59Ibid., p. 375.

60Moltmann does not deal with the "person and work" of the risen Christ in *The Crucified God*.

61Pannenberg, *Jesus*, p. 141.   62Ibid., p. 150.

63Ibid. Moltmann does not deal with the birth narratives.

64Cf. Moltmann, *Crucified God*, p. 204: "All Christian statements about history, about the church, about faith and sanctification, about the future and about hope stem from the crucified Christ."

Chapter 5

LIBERATION CHRISTOLOGY AND ITS CRITICS

This chapter is concerned with selected non-Latin American criticism of liberation Christology. The official Roman Catholic response has two parts: The first consists of selected speeches and sermons of John Paul II concerning liberation theology, and the second is found in the two instructions published by The Sacred Congregation for the Doctrine of the Faith. The Protestant response has three parts: that of Schubert M. Ogden, who represents the liberal Protestant response, that of Clark H. Pinnock, who represents the Evangelical response, and the third is the criticism of the writer.

Official Roman Catholic Responses

The official Roman Catholic criticism of liberation theology is voluminous. Unfortunately, little attention has been directed toward liberation Christology; therefore, this writer has taken it upon himself to apply these criticisms to the subject at hand.

Pope John Paul II

In 1986, Pope John Paul II told the Brazilian bishops "that, 'purified of elements that could adulterate it, with grave consequences for the faith, this theology of liberation is not only orthodox but necessary.'"[1] John Paul bases his criticism of liberation Christology upon the truth about the Church's mission, the truth about human beings, and the truth about Jesus Christ.[2] Therefore, it is necessary to examine these truths before turning to his critique.

First, evangelization is "the essential mission, the specific vocation" of the Church. As such, it is accomplished in community. Thus, evangelization requires "prompt, sincere respect for the sacred magisterium" which proclaims "the authentic word of God." This understanding of the Church's mission will correct two problems in liberation theology. One, there will not be a radical distinction between the Church and the kingdom of God. Too often, liberation theology posits a mere secular understanding of the kingdom. It maintains that:

> we do not arrive at the Kingdom through faith and membership in the Church but rather merely by structural change and sociopolitical involvement. When there is a certain kind of commitment and praxis for justice, there the kingdom is already present.[3]

These theologians forget that the Church's mission is to establish the kingdom among the nations; that the Church is the "initial budding forth" of the kingdom. Salvation in Jesus Christ and socio-political and economic liberation are not synonymous. Two, there will not be a dichotomy between the "institutional" or "official" Church and a "people's" Church. Vatican II has settled the matter: there is but one Church. If it appears divided, then "'those to whom we address our preaching [will] be disturbed, disoriented, and even scandalized.'"4

Secondly, the truth about human beings cannot be reduced to philosophical principles or political activity. The world has forgotten what the Church has always known; namely, that "the human being is the image of God and cannot be reduced to a mere fragment of nature or to an anonymous element in the human city."5 To announce this truth is the Church's duty. To fulfill this duty, the Church will:

> preach, educate persons and groups, shape public opinion, and give direction to national officials. . . . Eventually the Christian evangelical principle will lead to a more just and equitable distribution of goods, not only within each nation but also in the wide world as a whole.6

This means that economic and political processes are the servants of human beings, not vice versa. Bishops, therefore, must be on guard concerning the denial of the truth of human dignity. They must advocate the individual's right to freedom; to worship; to full psychosomatic well-being; to life and its necessities; to full participation in cultural, political, and economic structures; and to the annihilation of coercion and torture. The Church does not need "ideological systems" to defend and promote human dignity, for "violence, power plays, [and] political systems" do not liberate. The Church's truth does.7

Thirdly, the truth about Jesus Christ is found in Peter's confession at Caesarea Philippi: "You are the Christ, the Son of the living God" (Mt. 16:16). Adherence to this confession will guard against two dangers which are false "'rereadings'" of the gospel. The first is a lack of emphasis, even silence, concerning the divinity of Christ. The second danger is a conception of Jesus as a political activist.8

Adherence to this confession also has a positive role. Quoting Paul VI, John Paul urges the bishops to:

> 'take a position . . . for the defense and elucidation of the truths of the faith, on the relevance of the Gospel, on the questions that interest the life of the faithful and the defense of Christian conduct.'9

John Paul goes on to say: "To [Christ's] saving power open the boundaries of State, economic and political systems, the vast fields of culture, civilization, and development."10 As in the case of the Church's teaching about its mission and about human beings, the truth about Jesus Christ is holistic. All aspects of life constitute the Church's domain; but the entry point is the spiritual aspect: conversion is the Church's first priority.11

Based upon these truths, John Paul's criticism of liberation theology is both negative and positive. His negative criticism is a methodological one, which was hinted at in his warnings concerning "ideological systems" and "rereadings" of the gospel. In a nutshell, the issue is the use of Marxist analysis by liberation theologians, especially the concept of "class struggle." Indirectly, he acknowledges that class struggle is concerned with oppression and injustice. If human beings are the center of one's actions, all injustices are called into question. If injustice goes unchecked, society will be destroyed from within; but class struggle cannot bring about justice.[12] Instead of establishing justice, it transforms the disenfranchised into the privileged thereby creating a new situation of injustice.[13] The assumption here is that class struggle necessarily entails violence.

In spite of the fact that the reasons some liberation theologians advocate class struggle are valid, class struggle must be rejected.[14] For a just society to endure, the necessary transformations must come from "peaceful reforms," from effective action that is "often gradual and progressive." According to John Paul, peaceful reform is the duty of everyone: "All power finds its justification only in the common good, in achieving a just social order."[15] Peaceful reform results from cooperation among the power centers of society in behalf of the poor. If their situation is improved, everyone benefits.[16]

A corollary to this criticism is John Paul's understanding that liberation theologians rely upon economic reform to establish justice. To be sure, the economic sphere plays an important role in the criticism of an unjust status quo; but he understands them to be trusting "solely in the economic laws of growth . . . for regulating the domain of the distribution of goods."[17] He continues by saying that to believe solutions to social problems:

> will flow naturally from a kind of automatic extension of a certain economic order is not realistic, and therefore is not admissible. The economy will be viable only if it is human, for man and through man.[18]

Latin American priests and religious are often at the forefront of agitating for socio-political and economic transformation. For John Paul, in doing so, they are overstepping their authority. He exhorts them to:

> leave political responsibilities to those charged with them. . . . Your sphere of intervention . . . is that of faith and morals, where it is expected that you preach at the same time by a courageous word and by the example of your life.[19]

The priests' primary duties are the preaching of the whole gospel alongside the celebration of the sacraments. Priests, however, are to practice the art of discernment; they must be able to detect "ideological and psuedo-values" that are not consistent with the social teaching of the Church. An important part of discernment is the ability to teach "the faithful" how to make similar decisions on their own.[20]

Once Marxism has been ferreted out of liberation theology, it becomes clear that John Paul is at one with the goal of liberation theology. In a word, it is humanization, that is, the truth that all human beings are created in the image of God and worthy of respect, regardless of whether or not they are poor. The basis for this belief is his interpretation of the Beatitudes, especially Matthew 5:3: "Blessed are the poor in spirit for theirs is the kingdom of God." According to John Paul, "poor in spirit" may refer to spiritual poverty, physical poverty, or both. If one is poor in spirit, then one fulfills the rest of the Beatitudes: one hungers for justice; is afflicted; is a peacemaker; is merciful. A scandal arises when "poor in spirit" refers to the materially poor, for it does not erase the problem of poverty; instead, the problem is magnified. Therefore, if one is not poor in spirit, if one does not embody the Beatitudes, one will hear Christ's rebuke, "Woe to you."[21]

Since "poor in spirit" may have either a spiritual or physical connotation, its message is dependent upon its audience. To the rich and "the well off," "poor in spirit" is a call to conversion of "heart and conscience." Otherwise, "a just and stable social order is impossible."[22] This type of conversion is a both-and proposition. On the one hand, the privileged should reap the benefits of their work and enjoy their abundance. On the other hand, they are not to forget the poor. To the rich, John Paul applies the adage: "To whom much is given, much is required." Their socio-economic power, abilities, and education are to be used to serve others; human dignity is measured in quality, not quantity.[23]

That human dignity is qualitative and not quantitative is the beginning of the message of "poor in spirit" for the poor, although it leads in a very different direction. Once human dignity is recognized as a quality of life rather than quantity of goods, the poor begin to realize they can care for themselves, their families, and society.[24] John Paul, realizing that the poor cannot do this alone, maintains that "the prime and fundamental preoccupation of all, of those in government, politicians, labor union leaders, and owners of enterprises, ought to be to give work to all."[25] Thus, all people will understand "that it is not permissible . . . for anyone--to be reduced arbitrarily to misery"; in fact, it is "necessary" to do everything "licit" to avoid misery or to escape it.[26]

The "church of the poor" has the obligation of announcing this two-pronged message. According to John Paul, the "church of the poor" is "the universal church . . . not the church of one single class or one single race."[27] This Church will not serve "political purposes or power struggles," nor will it allow its words to be manipulated for such purposes. The church of the poor will, however, fight for "truth and justice" with a word of encouragement or of warning, whichever is appropriate.[28] The goal is a dynamic, "socially just society." As John Paul says: "Only a socially just society, one that strives to be ever more just, has a reason to exist."[29]

The Church's role in this process is to show the way to build the "earthly city," that is, a society fit for human beings. It does this by collaborating:

in the construction of . . . society, by discerning and nourishing the aspirations for justice and peace that it finds . . . with its wisdom and its effort to promote such aspirations.[30]

The Church's discernment and nourishment of these aspirations stems from its message of salvation, which is one of "love and fraternity . . . of justice and solidarity . . . for the most needy";[31] it is not, however, a static principle. It grows and changes with each new socio-political situation; but it is always characterized by justice.[32]

In light of the Church's position vis-à-vis the common good, Christians have the "right and duty" to participate in the building up of society. They are to support, in a knowledgeable and responsible way, reforms that are based upon Christian principles, justice, and an "authentic social ethic." John Paul believes this path of reform will avoid violence and the suppression of human rights and liberties.[33] Among the most important rights are the right "to life, to security, to work, to a home, to health, to education, to religious expression, both public and private, to participation [in the life of society]."[34]

The clergy is not exempt from participation in the common good, because:

evangelization, the Church's reason for being . . . would not be complete unless it took into account the relations existing between the gospel message and man's personal and social living, between the commandment to love one's suffering and needy neighbor, and concrete situations where injustice must be combated and justice and peace installed.[35]

Thus, it is the right and duty of the Church "to promote a social pastorate, that is, to exert an influence, through the means proper to it," on all of society.[36] The operative thought here is "through the means proper to it." As stated above, John Paul does not want the Church's ministers encumbered with political office. Their role is to support:

the spiritual and moral bases of society by doing what is possible for all or any activity in the field of the common good, carried out in harmony and coherence with the distinctives and demands of a human and Christian ethic.[37]

In conclusion, John Paul II is in fundamental agreement with liberation Christology. His "truth about human beings" parallels the liberation concern for the recognition of the humanity of the poor and oppressed it sees in Jesus' praxis. John Paul's concept of the "common good," of society based on love and justice, echoes the explication of Jesus' proclamation of the kingdom of God in liberation Christology. On the other hand, John Paul does not accept the use of Marxist analysis by liberation theologians. From his experience of Marxism in his native Poland, class struggle is permeated with violence and is characterized by the suppression of human rights. Thus, he advocates reform of the status quo rather than its transformation by revolution.

Sacred Congregation for the
Doctrine of the Faith

Liberation theology began to be scrutinized in the early 1980s, which is evidenced by the Sacred Congregation for the Doctrine of the Faith issuing two works dealing with the subject.38 The purpose of the first *Instruction* is:

> to draw . . . attention . . . to the deviations, and risks of deviations . . . that are brought about by certain forms of liberation theology which use, in an insufficiently critical manner, concepts borrowed from various currents of marxist [*sic*] thought.39

This statement should not be interpreted as being against the "preferential option for the poor," a major theme of liberation theology; nor is it a defense for "neutrality and indifference" vis-à-vis injustice. It is an explication of the way the Church advocates justice "by her own means."40

The purpose of the second *Instruction* is to "highlight the main elements of the Christian doctrine on freedom and liberation."41 As such, it does not exhaust the subject; rather, it is limited to the "principal *theoretical* and *practical* aspects" of Christian freedom and liberation. It is left up to the local churches, "in communion with one another and with the See of Peter," to apply them to specific situations.42

The congregation's fundamental negative criticism of liberation theology is a methodological one. Succinctly stated, the use of Marxist social analysis by liberation theologians, as the most effective one, needs to be re-examined. According to the congregation, Marx's thought is a "global vision" that prioritizes the "significance and importance" of the data brought to it. Thus, Marxist ideology cannot be divided into parts; one either accepts it or rejects it. This is based on the position of Paul VI in his *Octogesima Adveniens*, that Marxism, as it is lived today, is incompatible with the Church's teachings. One cannot incorporate into theology an analysis that is based upon "atheism and the denial of the human person, his liberty, and his rights."43 "It is the light of faith" which determines what may be borrowed from other disciplines.44

The adoption of Marxist analysis by liberation theologians brings a new hermeneutical principle to theology: class struggle. What results is a "*political* re-reading" of Scripture. The mistake is not the recognition of the political overtones of Scripture, but occurs when class struggle, understood as "the fundamental law of history," is made *the* lens through which Scripture is read.45

The theological ramifications of this hermeneutic are multitude and disastrous. First, revolution is viewed as a viable means for attaining liberation. Even when this is not the case, revolutionary language is still employed as a tool for communication. Second, the belief that love can conquer evil is an illusion; this can only happen through "revolutionary *praxis*." Third, the eternal kingdom of God is equated with temporal human liberation movements; history is a process of self-redemption through class struggle. God is often identified with history, faith with "fidelity to history," hope with "confidence in the future," and charity with the "option for the poor." Fourth, faith is subjected to the "political criterion" of class struggle for verification. Finally, love, as a positive virtue, is extended to some (the poor) and not to others (the rich).46

The christological effects of this hermeneutic are equally devastating, resulting in a fundamental misunderstanding of Christ and of the salvation he offered. For the congregation, Jesus Christ is "true God and true man"; the salvation he offers "is above all liberation from sin, which is the source of all evils."[47] According to their reading of liberation theology, Chalcedon reveals a "Jesus of history" in solidarity with the revolution of the poor. Therefore, participation in revolution is living a life analogous to that of Jesus. Then, and only then, is knowledge of the true God and of God's kingdom revealed. Thus:

> faith in the Incarnate Word, dead and risen for all . . . whom "God made Lord and Christ" is denied. In its place is substituted a figure of Jesus who is a kind of symbol who sums up in Himself the requirements of the struggle of the oppressed.[48]

Second, Jesus' death is depicted as an exclusively political event that denies its validity for "the whole economy of redemption."[49]

Ecclesiology also suffers from the hermeneutic of class struggle. The Church is divided into warring camps and becomes a mere historical phenomenon. The "church of the poor" is a class church which confuses the poor with the proletariat. Thus, it becomes "a challenge to the *sacramental and hierarchical structure* of the Church" itself. If the hierarchy and magisterium are not partisan in behalf of the poor, they are regarded as part of the ruling class to be opposed.[50] The Eucharist is not "the gift of the Body and Blood of Christ," but "a celebration of the people in their struggle."[51]

This attack on the magisterium stems from a misunderstanding of its stance vis-à-vis liberation movements. According to the congregation, the magisterium supports reform movements because they do not entail violence and the suppression of rights. This means that the magisterium speaks against movements that it believes would ultimately thwart freedom, for example, violent revolutions and movements using aspects of Marxist thought. Because the magisterium does both, it is often viewed as an obstacle to freedom. The congregation admits the Church made mistakes in the past; but they are the exception rather than the rule. Freedom will come if the magisterial teachings are followed because the various parts of the economy of redemption will receive their correct emphasis. In other words, once the individual is changed, the ethical dimensions of salvation become clear.[52] The assumption here is that as the behaviors and attitudes of individuals change, the structure of society will reflect this change.

The correct way to accomplish this is for the Church to address injustice in light of the Beatitudes, that is, "in her own way." Echoing John Paul II, the Church's defense of justice is based on "the truth of mankind, created in the image of God and called to the grace of divine sonship."[53] In other words, orthodoxy precedes orthopraxy. The need to reform social structures should not blind people to the fact that the "source of injustice" lies in the "hearts of men": social change results from "interior conversion."[54] The assumption here is that:

> Liberation is first and foremost liberation from radical slavery to sin. . . . As a logical consequence, it calls for freedom from many different kinds of slavery in the cultural, economic, social and political spheres, all of which derive ultimately from sin . . . .[55]

The congregation concludes from this that it is "necessary to work simultaneously" for individual conversion and social transformation.56

Therefore, the correct way to change the world involves four steps. The first step is to give proper appreciation to the "*social teachings of the church*."57 Adherence to these teachings is a dynamic process which sets the parameters of Christian praxis and social work. Second, suggestions "from the field" are welcome. These contributions are valid only if their praxis is within the parameters of the Church's social teaching, which is to say, the first priority is conversion. The third step is for pastors to cultivate laypeople who will "build society" in the fields of science and technology as well as in the human and political fields. The fourth step refers specifically to the Latin American phenomenon of the base communities. These communities should catechize from the perspective of the "*whole message of salvation*" to liberative practice; orthodoxy has precedence over orthopraxy. If these four steps are followed, then the deviations of liberation theology will be overcome.58

The positive aspect of the congregation's critique is evident in that it concurs with liberation theology concerning the biblical basis of liberation. It states that liberation is a major motif of covenantal theology. The Exodus, Law, and prophets are based upon the religious and political duality of the Sinaitic covenant. The fulfillment of this covenant arrived when "the children of Abraham were invited to enter, together with all the nation, into the Church of Christ in order to form with them one People of God, spiritual and universal."59

Jesus, a poor man, extended this invitation and found an audience in the poor; but, the congregation says, he "wished to be near" the rich, also. This indicates that his mission was primarily spiritual in nature. Even so, this does not erase the fact that poverty is the result of sin and is, therefore, an evil to be eradicated. The Church attempts to follow his example. Its "special option for the poor, far from being a sign of particularism or sectarianism, manifests the universality of the Church's being and mission. This option excludes no one."60 The evil of poverty taints both the poverty-stricken and the rich; therefore, both groups need to hear the fullness of the gospel.

Christ's freedom means that love has no limits. Merciful love was the reason that the rich were castigated. Merciful love is the reason why love of God must be accompanied by love of neighbor. Practically speaking, love and justice go together. Living in this freedom is living in the hope of the Second Coming of Christ and the establishment of God's kingdom. This hope does not negate temporal life, but it does place it in the proper perspective: temporal life does not "belong to the same order" as eternal life. This statement does not mean there is a separation between the temporal and the eternal, only a distinction.61 In other words, the two are related but are not the same.

In conclusion, the Sacred Congregation for the Doctrine of the Faith is more critical of liberation Christology than was John Paul II. The congregation agreed with his criticism of liberation theology's use of Marxist analysis. The basis for its position was the violence that accompanies the use of class struggle to interpret social reality. The congregation also criticized the reinterpretation of

Chalcedon in liberation Christology. It understood this reinterpretation to be the result of Marxist analysis rather than theological necessity. The congregation disagreed with the interpretation of Jesus' death as a political event rather than a soteriological one. Again, this position was taken because this political interpretation came from the hermeneutic of class struggle rather than biblical exegesis and Church tradition. On the other hand, the congregation agreed that liberation is an important biblical motif. Thus, it supports liberation theology's "preferential option for the poor," alongside a more positive approach to those who are not oppressed. This writer believes the congregation's instructions would have been different if it had taken into consideration the christological writings of Boff and Sobrino. Its fear of reductionism, of the politicization of Jesus and the Church, would have been eased, if not eliminated.

Selected Protestant Responses

This section is concerned with selected Protestant responses to liberation Christology. Schubert M. Ogden represents liberal Protestantism, while Clark H. Pinnock represents the Evangelicals. The chapter concludes with a critique by the writer.

Schubert M. Ogden

Schubert M. Ogden is University Distinguished Professor of Theology, and the Director of the Graduate Department of Religious Studies at Southern Methodist University in Dallas, Texas. His criticism of liberation Christology is the fourth chapter of his book, *Faith and Freedom*.[62]

Ogden's critique of liberation Christology is based upon his assertion that "Jesus Christ is the decisive re-presentation of freedom."[63] He unpacks this statement in the form of five points. First, to be human is to be self-consciously existent vis-à-vis other people and the whole of reality that is the source and end of all. Second, this general understanding of existence is "re-presented" by "the explicit conceptualization and symbolization of the complex reality" that, to some degree, must be understood. Third, this means one's understanding of existence is culture specific. In other words, this specific understanding of existence enables a re-presentation of one's "existence with others under the gift and demand of God," "God" being one way to conceive and symbolize ultimate reality. The next point posits an innate religiosity in human beings, though this phenomenon takes different forms. The final point is that these forms of religiosity raise the question of "*the* religion," of the decisive re-presentation of human existence that is the norm for deciding between the conflicting truth claims of different religions.[64]

From these five points, Ogden concludes that:

the event of Jesus Christ is the re-presentation of our ultimate possibility in the face of the encompassing mystery of our existence as the possibility of freedom--of existence *in* freedom and *for* freedom--and of this mystery itself, correspondingly, as the pure unbounded love that is the only conceivable ground of this freedom.[65]

Based upon this understanding of Christology, Ogden's negative criticisms of liberation Christology are concerned with the meaning of the phrase "Jesus is the Christ," liberation Christology's relationship to the historical Jesus, and its concept of "Jesus as the way to God."

For Ogden, "Jesus is the Christ" is the answer to Jesus' question, "Who do you say I am?" This answer means that:

> the event to which its subject term "Jesus" refers is the event in which the gift and demand of radical freedom, which are implicitly presented to our existence in all times and places through our implicit self-understanding simply as human beings, are also made fully explicit in concepts and symbols, and thus decisively re-presented.[66]

This Jesus is not the historical Jesus that liberation Christology, and most modern Christologies, find in the Gospels. Since apostolicity was the criterion used to form the canon, the norm of Christology should be the apostolic witness, that is, "Jesus is the Christ," not the man whose history may be reconstructed from the Gospels. The Jesus of the apostolic witness is not the person "*with* whom" one believes in God; rather, he is the one "*through* whom" one believes in God.[67]

Thus, Ogden disagrees with Sobrino's assertion of "Jesus as the way to God," "way" understood as a road to be traveled, as stated above in the third chapter. At no point, Ogden says, did the New Testament base its assertion that "Jesus is the Christ" on Jesus' own faith, or that he lived faith in its pristine fullness. The closest the New Testament comes to this is Hebrews 12:2, a passage Sobrino refers to constantly. According to Ogden, the subject of this passage is "our faith," not Jesus'. Ogden concludes that the early church was not interested in Jesus' faith, but only in his being the origin, principle, and authorizing source of their faith. The same holds true for references to Jesus' love and obedience. The early church was bearing witness to its own faith, not relating historical facts that are the basis of its faith. Thus, there is no reason to infer that "Jesus is the Christ" because he perfectly lived the life of faith. To do so would be a "projection" of what Christian existence in freedom would be from a supposed "christological foundation."[68]

A corollary to this criticism concerns the humanity and divinity of Jesus. Ogden asserts that the New Testament assumes the humanity of Jesus, along with all the implication of this assumption: Jesus believed in God, bore witness to God's kingdom, and so on. But the point of claiming that "Jesus is the Christ" is to place him on the divine side of the divine-human relationship. Ogden says it is "precisely as a human being that [Jesus] is understood to be the decisive re-presentation, and hence the real, sacramental presence of God to all humankind."[69] Ogden seems to be saying that it was the divinity of Jesus that was paramount for the apostolic witness. For the man Jesus to be "the real, sacramental presence of God," who is the all-encompassing mystery and ground of freedom, he had to be divine, also.

Ogden also criticizes liberation Christology's use of the Gospels and its concept of God. Regarding the former, liberation Christology bases its picture of Jesus primarily upon the Synoptics, supported by other passages throughout the New Testament. But Ogden does not locate this base in the Synoptics, for they themselves are interpretations of the apostolic witness to Christ. This witness is what Ogden, borrowing from Willi Marxsen, calls the "Jesus-kerygma." It is composed of the narrative pericopes in Mark and the so-called "Q" source. Ogden asserts that there is no explicit Christology present in this witness. Christology results from the church's reflection upon this witness. The apostolic witness to Jesus is one "in which he himself appears as a witness--not to himself but to the imminent coming of the reign of God, and to its present gift and demand."[70] In other words, the significance of Jesus is based upon his witness to God's kingdom.[71]

For Ogden, the fundamental problem of liberation Christology's doctrine of God is that it perpetuates "uncritically the well-known concept of God of classical metaphysics."[72] Ogden prefers a process model. He argues that:

> one may go so far as to say that process metaphysics is precisely *the* metaphysics of freedom, which insists on the applicability of its key concept to literally everything that can be actual at all, from the least particle of so-called physical matter to the God whom, in Anselm's words, "none greater can be conceived."[73]

Ogden's choice of a process model for God has two consequences. The first is a new understanding of the attributes of God. Omnipotence is redefined as all the power God could have in relationship to the lesser power of other beings. God is also "omnibeneficient," that is, God uses God's power for self-creation in order to optimize the potentialities of freedom of all other beings. Together, these two attributes of God set limits in order to actualize freedom for good rather than for evil. Second, all beings, including God, are partially determined by others. The difference between God and all other beings is that "God's is the one actual being" that partly determines all other beings. This is evidenced in God's being supreme love, the Redeemer and Emancipator who is the ground of freedom.[74]

Ogden supports liberation Christology at three points. The first concerns the purpose of liberation Christology. For Ogden, a liberation Christology:

> must be an attempt to understand the meaning of the Christian witness . . . to Jesus as the Christ--in terms of the question of men and women today concerning the nature of authentic freedom and its ultimate ground.[75]

This means several things. First, freedom and faith in Jesus Christ interpret one another, so that faith in Christ is the existence of freedom and "authentic existence of freedom" is faith in Christ. Second, salvation is defined by the "unique historical event of Jesus Christ," but is not confined to it. Ogden makes this distinction because when Christians were a minority, they were not exclusive. Third, to be a Christian is to be a sign of God's redeeming love. God's love is all-encompassing, and Christians are called to be faithful to the recipients of that love. Fourth, the church is the "primary sacrament" of God's love. It is not the only sacrament of God's love, but its sacramentality is unique in that it is a sacrament of "the only love that is . . . truly redeeming."[76]

Ogden's second point concerns the optimization of freedom. From a specifically human standpoint, "to be fully human is to be an active *subject* of historical change, not merely its passive *object*."[77] Therefore, faith in God is not only faithfulness to God, it is also faithfulness to all to whom God is faithful. Love is the criterion for judging faithfulness. If love is really present, then freedom will also be present. In this sense, love is both active and passive. If one loves another, one will act and speak in a way that will optimize the other's freedom. If one is loved, then one's freedom will be optimized by the way one is spoken to and acted upon. Thus, faith in God is existence in freedom and for freedom; faith is liberated and liberating.[78]

This intra-human action is reflective of the way God acts towards God's creatures. God exercises God's power in order to maximize the freedom for every being's self-creation. This is accomplished by the establishment of "fundamental limits of natural order" that incline the actualization of possibilities toward good rather than evil. Therefore, God is partisan; but God's partiality is to freedom rather than ideology. In other words, God's acceptance is not equal to God's approval. The former is determined by the "unsurpassable goodness" of God's intention for creation, namely, the optimization of freedom for good.[79]

Ogden's third point of agreement concerns social change, which he bases on the idea of God as Emancipator, the role "in which God is dependent on the co-operation of God's creatures" to optimize freedom for good. Human cooperation in this work requires laboring:

> for fundamental social and cultural change--the kind of structural or systemic change in the very order of our society and culture that is clearly necessary if each and every person is to be the active subject of his or her history instead of merely its passive object.[80]

To speak of such change is to speak of the "necessarily conflictive character" of human existence; partiality is the responsibility of human beings as well as God.[81]

This labor may be an explicitly Christian witness in the form of religious words and deeds; but it may also be an implicitly Christian witness through every nonreligious word and deed. This view presupposes that a society's values are expressed in its culture (politics, morality, arts, and technology) as well as its religion(s).[82] Thus, both forms of witness are valid for Christians. Ogden's point is that, together, they constitute all that a Christian ought to do.[83]

In conclusion, Ogden criticizes liberation Christology at three points. First, he rejects the contention that Jesus is the one "*through* whom" and "*with* whom" on believes in God. For Ogden, only the former has scriptural support. Second, Ogden criticizes liberation Christology for basing its interpretation of Jesus upon the Synoptic Gospels rather than the "apostolic witness" itself, of which they are an interpretation. Third, Ogden critiques liberation theology's concept of God. For him, the God of "classical metaphysics" is unable to be a liberating God. He contends that the God of process theology is better suited for a theology of liberation. Ogden is supportive of the use of the concept of liberation as being credible and appropriate to today's socio-political reality. He also affirms the social consciousness that is inherent in the desire for human liberation.

Clark H. Pinnock

One is hard pressed to find an Evangelical critique of liberation Christology.[84] Most Evangelical critiques focus on liberation theology's affiliation with Marxism, thereby giving liberation Christology a mere tip of the hat.[85] The best example is that of Clark H. Pinnock. Even though he offers only an "outline of a systematic theology for public discipleship," his systematic approach provides the grist for a critique of liberation Christology.[86]

Assuming that Pinnock's methodology is found in his ordering of theological topics, his negative criticism begins with methodology. Instead of a social analysis, he begins with revelation and the authority of Scripture. According to him, "biblical people" begin with the Bible, the record of God's self-revelation culminating in the Incarnation. This methodology allows Christians to avoid being "swallowed up in the sinful and relative human situation," that is, their culture and ideological beliefs. To be sure, the contemporary human situation must be analyzed and understood before the gospel may be applied to it; but social analysis is not theological data. The latter derives only from Scripture.[87]

Pinnock also criticizes liberation Christology as a Christology "from below." For him, "the heart of the gospel is the claim that God himself was present in Jesus Christ."[88] Thus, the emphasis is upon the divinity of Jesus. The result is that Pinnock discusses the significance of Jesus Christ under the heading "God the Son" rather than "the Person of Jesus Christ.

Pinnock's third criticism is directly related to the first one: liberation theologians have a faulty doctrine of sin. Their idealization of the proletariat blinds them to the presence of sin among the poor and oppressed. As Pinnock says: "All people, whatever their class or station, can be treacherous and selfish, stupid and lazy, aggressive and destructive."[89] This idealization also ignores the fact that eschatological fulfillment entails both liberation and judgment. Even though Pinnock directs this thought to North American churches, the implication of universal human sinfulness is that the oppressed will receive God's judgment as well as God's liberation.[90]

Another criticism is the absence of an ecological concern in liberation Christology. A major part of the oppression experienced by Latin America is the depletion of its natural resources and raw materials by multinational corporations. Pinnock's point is that the common good is being destroyed by "a system of legal injustice" for the benefit of a few.[91] In other words, if liberation is ever achieved, it will be of little benefit for the poor because they will have no natural resources with which to build their new society.

Pinnock also commends liberation Christology at several points. The first stems from the way Jesus lived his life, that is, as a servant. According to Pinnock: "The quality of his humanity according to the New Testament can be characterized as obedient servanthood, obedient to the will of his Father, and radically open to the needs of people."[92] This is a surprising turn of events because: 1) Jesus is God incarnate, and 2) because this lifestyle is truly "radically counter-cultural."[93] This servant paradigm means Jesus' call to discipleship is a summons for people to live in a manner "completely contrary to life . . . in the old age." That is to say, to live a life that is partial to the poor and needy; to seek to implement justice; and the well-being of God's creation.[94]

For Christians to live as servants, Pinnock advocates a critical stance vis-à-vis the State. On the one hand, the State is good because it gives order to human life and society. On the other hand, it is a part of the fallen structure of human life.[95] Christians must be involved in the affairs of the State in order to discern whether or not the political and economic structures in which they participate are "humane and fair." Since these structures are an outgrowth of fallen humanity, Pinnock contends "it would be wrong not to press for systemic change if it seemed urgent and the way was open to do so."[96] Pinnock also agrees with liberation Christology that Jesus' crucifixion is the result of his praxis. By refusing to submit to the religious and political power brokers of his day, Jesus "accepted the penalty they prescribed for those who dare to place their loyalty elsewhere."[97] Through this act of "powerlessness," God broke the power of religious and political oppression that separated people from God. By this act, God simultaneously established the "ethical paradigm for Christian conduct." Christian behavior is "now defined in terms of self-giving love and neighbor-oriented service."[98]

The primary import of the resurrection is the vindication of Jesus. Pinnock speaks of this primarily in relation to the scandal of the crucifixion; but because of his description of why Jesus was crucified, he implies that the resurrection is also the vindication of Jesus' life and message. Therefore, the resurrection is also the "pre-actualizing of the end": Jesus is the first fruits of the kingdom of God.[99] The resurrection engenders hope in Christians, and "whets our appetite for more newness . . . for all of God's creation, and it inspires us to throw all our energies into the divine work of healing and renewal."[100]

Pinnock also affirms with liberation Christology that the Christian life is communal as well as individual. Individual Christians are part of "a new community filled with the Spirit and intended to serve as an agency through which God . . . [overcomes] our bondage, enabling us to become what God originally intended."[101] Thus, Christian discipleship is not purely an individual quest. It also concerns the whole community. This implies an expansion of the concept of "Christian holiness." On the one hand, it is a change in an individual's attitudes and actions. On the other hand, it is a "spirituality of liberation" in which Christians commit themselves to the liberation of the oppressed. This spirituality takes seriously God's "passion for justice" and creatively seeks to actualize it.[102] Pinnock concludes that "our conversion to Christ involves a conversion to the needy neighbor."[103]

The preeminence of eschatology, understood as "the ultimate consummation of God's purposes for history," is another point where Pinnock agrees with liberation Christology. God's purpose for history is nothing less than God's kingdom. Christians, as members of the new community, live their lives in the old age according to the demands of the coming new age. This has two important ramifications. First, the onus of success is lifted from the shoulders of Christians because they confess faith in Jesus, "the firstborn from the dead."[104] Second, history is the arena for "the outworking of God's purposes for human life. . . . The sacred/secular dichotomy is invalid."[105] All human activities and tasks are embodiments of service, for all of human life stands under the judgment of God.[106]

This writer noted, with some surprise, that Pinnock referred to Marx about as often as did Boff and Sobrino. Throughout both articles Pinnock emphasized the social character of theological concepts; something that Evangelicals usually ignore. Pinnock also questions the "right of private property," an obvious allusion to Marx's own critique of this subject.[107] Of the three times he specifically mentions Marx, two are in a positive light. The first relates to eschatology: the Christian hope in God's kingdom "places us more in a class with Marxists" than with their Western secular contemporaries who are more Epicurean in their eschatology.[108] The second refers to Marx's "searching criticism" of religion as the opiate of the people. For Pinnock, a truly "biblical religion" is not a drug, but a source of liberation, which was the point of Marx's criticism.[109] Pinnock's only negative reference to Marx was his critique of the "ideologizing [of] the proletariat," noted above.[110]

In conclusion, Pinnock is critical of liberation Christology at several points. First, he does not accept social analysis as theological data. For him, the latter is derived only from Scripture. Second, he is critical of liberation Christology as a Christology "from below." He contends that Christology begins with the incarnation of the eternal Son of God. A corollary to this is his contention that liberation theology has a faulty doctrine of sin: it acts as if sin does not transcend economic and class lines. Fourth, Pinnock criticizes the lack of an ecological concern in liberation Christology. He also praises several aspects of liberation Christology. He commends their presentation of Jesus as a servant. He, too, advocates a critical stance toward political structures, though not to the extent liberation theologians do. Pinnock argues, with liberation Christology, that Jesus' death resulted from his lifestyle. Thus, the resurrection was God's vindication of Jesus' life and ministry. Pinnock affirms the contention that the Christian life is both communal and individual. Finally, he is in fundamental agreement with liberation Christology concerning the preeminence of eschatology, of the kingdom of God, for Christology.

Author's Response

The final section of this chapter is this writer's response to liberation Christology. The areas being analyzed are: 1) the role and interpretation of Scripture; 2) the role of christological tradition; and 3) the recognition of contextuality.

Role and Interpretation
of Scripture

That Scripture plays a major role in liberation Christology cannot be denied. Its emphasis upon the historical Jesus requires a critical examination of the Gospels, which raises the question of the nature of biblical authority. This issue is not addressed directly by Boff nor by Sobrino; however, one may infer from their use of historical criticism that they do not adhere to a literal interpretation of Scripture; however, they accept the biblical witness to Jesus as trustworthy. If this were not the case, there would be no need for the amount of exegesis present in their Christologies; they would not need to appeal to Scripture for their perception of Jesus as "the Liberator." But their "faith" in the Bible is not due to its inspiration, infallibility, or canonicity. It exists because the scriptural witness to Jesus has been verified in the lives of Christians down through history.

The authority of Scripture is only one facet of the role Scripture plays in liberation Christology. Another facet is its place in the hermeneutic circle. The reader will remember from the first chapter that this circle revolves around the two foci of present day reality and the Bible. To this writer, which of these focal points comes first is a moot question, for both impact the other. The Bible is interpreted in light of one's experience of reality. Likewise, one's perception of reality is simultaneously colored by one's understanding of Scripture. This is not a denigration of the authority of Scripture, only a recognition of the way things are.

Therefore, the Bible functions as the source of information about the life, message, and praxis of Jesus of Nazareth for liberation Christology. On this point, liberation Christology is in agreement with its contemporaries. This has two implications. First, Scripture is the basis for the dialogue between liberation Christology and other modern Christologies. Since they share a common source, their continuities and discontinuities are more readily recognized and clarified. Second, criticism of liberation Christology's presentation of Jesus must be scripturally based. Liberation Christology is not the result of the imposition of Marxist ideology upon the Bible; it is not eisegesis; rather, it is the interpretation of the Gospel record applied to the Latin American situation.

The interpretation of Scripture within liberation Christology is a different matter. The major difference lies in its explicit recognition of its presuppositions. In other words, no one reads the Bible objectively, as if one's mind is a *tabula rasa* vis-à-vis Holy Writ. Denominational heritage, class, race, sex, and experience (both individual and collective) color one's interpretation; therefore, to interpret Scripture from the perspective of liberation is natural and correct in light of the Latin American experience of colonialism, oppression, and underdevelopment. Likewise, to call Jesus "the Liberator," and to view his life and message as liberative, is also natural and correct. This raises the issue of the relationship between liberation Christology and other contemporary Christologies, which will be discussed below under contextuality. Suffice it to say at this point that, considering its biblical and modern sources, liberation Christology is a valid and viable Christology for Latin America.

Role of Christological
 Tradition

To be honest, the christological councils have not played an explicit role in this writer's Christian pilgrimage; but after studying them, he is in agreement with the presentation of them in liberation Christology: they are historical manifestations of some aspect of the Christian faith. This has two implications. On the one hand, they should, and do, have an impact on Christology today. On the other hand, they are less than Scripture, both in comprehensiveness and worth. Therefore, their value is not denied if one takes a critical stance toward them.

One aspect of such a stance is a truism, but it bears repeating: the languages and the mindset of the Mediterranean Sea area in the fifth century C.E. are not the same as those present in twentieth century Latin America. At the most fundamental level this fact calls for translation; which necessarily involves interpretation. Therefore, liberation Christology is not out of line when it calls for a reinterpretation of Chalcedon, the watershed of the christological councils.

Another aspect of this stance toward christological creeds relates to history: they have been lifted out of their historical contexts and transformed into timeless dogmas. The centuries that preceded them, their protagonists, the "political" maneuvering, even Scripture itself, seem irrelevant to their exalted position. Liberation Christology, by critically evaluating the creeds, attempts to return them to their historical contexts. This accomplishes two things. First, it reveals the struggles of a living church to understand its faith, its mission, and itself. Second, it reveals the dynamic nature of Christian faith. Therefore, liberation Christology is being faithful to history in its attempt to formulate a Christology relevant to Latin America.

The final aspect of this critical stance is methodological: Christology "from above" is not a viable option for Latin America. The reason for this is simple: it is too easy to forget the reality of the present: oppression, underdevelopment, and death; but when Christology proceeds "from below," reality is paramount. The world that surrounded Jesus helped form his person and his message. He spoke to his listeners in their language and in ways they could understand. Likewise, the world surrounding Jesus' disciples have impacted their message and their presentation of it since that time. Liberation Christology is consciously following that example.

To conclude, liberation Christology is completely orthodox in its proclamation of Jesus as truly divine and truly human. Finite human language is incapable of plumbing the depths as to the way this is possible. Nevertheless, the attempt must be made. But the dogmatization, in a pejorative sense, of any assertion as to the way Jesus is both divine and human causes Christology as a whole to stagnate and become irrelevant. Then it dies, casting aspersions upon the whole christological endeavor. By following the spirit of Chalcedon, liberation Christology strikes a balance between orthodoxy and relevancy.

Recognition of
Contextuality

The recognition of the contextual nature of theology is one of liberation theology's greatest strengths. This, however, has always been the case; but the lure of objectivity, with its promise to be *the* theology of the ages, has blinded theologians to the obvious for centuries. One reason for this situation is the equating of subjectivity with relativity. The issue at stake is the existence of norms, constants, or absolutes. Subjectivity relates to a person's or group's experience and understanding of norms or constants. Relativity assumes there are no norms, or that they are entirely dependent upon the present situation alone. Liberation Christology is unashamedly subjective. As examined in this dissertation, some of its major norms are Jesus Christ, Scripture, ecumenical councils, the Church, and the experience of socio-economic and political oppression.

The question arises, then, as to what keeps the subjectivity of liberation Christology from becoming relativity. The answer is: the community. Community refers not only to the universality of the Roman Catholic Church, but it also refers to the base Christian communities, the grassroot communities within the Catholic churches of Latin America. The Christologies espoused by Boff and Sobrino grew out of these communities. In other words, liberation Christology is not the brainchild of isolated academicians throughout Latin America. They systematized the Christology that was being lived and thought out in those communities.

Another aspect of contextuality relates to the purpose of liberation Christology, which is found in the title of this dissertation: to make contributions to the field of Christology from the perspective of Latin American liberation theology. In doing so, it does not seek to supplant the christological work that has already been done; it seeks to complement that work by providing ways to overcome perceived deficiencies.

Therefore, an important aspect of contextuality is dialogue. The contextual nature of liberation Christology does not exclude insights from outside of Latin America. Both the theological training and the bibliography used by Boff and Sobrino support this. In other words, liberation Christology has shown that it can learn from voices that are not oppressed. What remains to be seen is if European and North American Christologies can learn from the oppressed. To date, North Atlantic Christology has not been very receptive to contributions from Latin America. This only reinforces the feeling among liberation theologians that North Atlantic theologians think that their theology is complete and, therefore, superior to liberation theology. Such an atmosphere is not conducive to dialogue. If this dissertation has helped to "clear the air" at all, then it will have been a worthwhile endeavor.

Conclusion

This chapter consists of selected critiques of liberation Christology. Even though they are representative of the whole church, their criticisms are not equal in value nor validity. Thus, the issue now is to evaluate the work of these critics.

The critique of John Paul II cannot be easily discounted, for he has provided a consistent, albeit, conservative treatment. He aligned himself with the major goals of liberation Christology: justice for all people, regardless of their socio-political status; recognition of the humanity of all persons; non-violent civil disobedience for the transformation of society; and a "preferential option for the poor." But he succumbs to the same problem as Wolfhart Pannenberg, that is, he rejects the use of Marxism by liberation theologians based upon his experience of communism in Eastern Europe. On the one hand, this is a valid criticism because it allows him to point to possible dangers and excesses that might arise from the use of Marxist analysis. On the other hand, this criticism is an invalid one for several reasons: 1) liberation theologians do not advocate coming under Soviet or Chinese domination; 2) he overlooks the fact that communism is not synonymous with socialism; and 3) there are ways to combine a socialist economic system with a democratic form of government.

Even though the Sacred Congregation for the Doctrine of the Faith's two instructions received the approval of John Paul II, it is easy to discount its critique because it is based upon a complete lack of understanding of liberation Christology.[113] In addition to this, the theologians criticized are not named; there are no references to any Latin American christological writings; and there are no citations given to enable one to check the congregation's interpretations. Since the congregation has not chosen to be theologically rigorous in its critique, one is led to the conclusion that its instructions are nothing but an exercise in authoritarianism: "This is the magisterium's position concerning liberation theology, therefore, all good Roman Catholics will abide by it." The only criticism with any validity is its rejection of Marxism. But the congregation merely echoes the reservations of John Paul II, along with his faulty presuppositions; thus, Marxism functions as a "straw man." At every critical juncture, that is, whenever the sociopolitical aspects of liberation Christology arise, the congregation cries, "Marxism!," and rejects the point *in toto*. Until the congregation issues an honest analysis of liberation theology, its criticism of liberation Christology cannot be taken seriously.

Schubert Ogden provides the most fruitful critique of liberation Christology. He actively engages the subject, via Sobrino's *Christology at the Crossroads*, which the other critics do not do. This engagement gives his criticisms more weight since his knowledge of the subject is more complete. Even so, his use of the "apostolic witness" as the basis of his criticisms is questionable. First, he presupposes that it, rather than the Gospels, is the norm for Christology. If it is, then this criticism may also be directed toward contemporary Christology at large. Second, his use of it to make a methodological critique is debatable because of its emphasis upon the divinity of Jesus, which is not consistent with his very human criterion that the gospel be "credible and appropriate" to the hopes and desires of women and men today. His criticism, however, of the traditional model of God, which liberation Christology accepts, is very intriguing. It would be cavalier to dismiss this as a mere cultural phenomenon resulting from the Enlightenment's emphasis upon human freedom, for the process model of God addresses issues that are at the heart of divine-human relationship. It remains to be seen whether or not this model can be appropriated by Latin Americans for their situation.[114]

Clark Pinnock appears to be one of those people who knows what he believes, dialogues from that position, yet leaves one wondering whether or not he accepts diversity of theological interpretation within the unity of the Christian faith. On the one hand, the points at which he agrees with liberation Christology indicate that he accepts this diversity since he arrives at these conclusions from a different perspective than Boff and Sobrino. On the other hand, he is a thorough-going evangelical when he disagrees with them. Based upon his own description of his theological pilgrimage and his role in "the battle for the Bible," one is forced to conclude that he does not accept diversity of this magnitude. In other words, liberation Christology is wrong because it differs from his perspective. Therefore, like the Sacred Congregation for the Doctrine of the Faith, Pinnock is authoritarian. But his authoritarianism resides in a literal interpretation of the Bible that equates unity with conformity and diversity with heresy. Until Pinnock broadens his horizons, his similarities with liberation Christology are nothing but the *noblesse oblige* of the self-proclaimed theological elite.

Notes

[1]Richard N. Ostling, "A Lesson on Liberation," *Time*, April 14, 1986, p. 84.

[2]Quentin L. Quade, ed., *The Pope and Revolution: John Paul II Confronts Liberation Theology* (Washington, D.C.: Ethics and Public Policy Center, 1982), p. 57. These truths were expounded in John Paul's opening address to CELAM III, January 28, 1979. Cited hereafter as *The Pope*.

[3]Ibid., p. 58. [4]Ibid., John Paul II quoting Paul VI. [5]Ibid., p. 49. [6]Ibid., p. 65.

[7]Ibid., pp. 59-65. John Paul also points out two "signs of true Christian liberation over against ideological liberation. The first is faithfulness to the Word of God, the church's living tradition, and the magisterium. The second is communion with the bishops and the rest of the People of God as confirmed by contribution to the edification of the community and service to the needy and oppressed."

[8]Quade, *The Pope*, p. 53. [9]Ibid., p. 55, quoting from his inaugural homily. [10]Ibid.

[11]See ibid., p. 67: Liberation is first and foremost liberation from sin. Spiritual liberation precedes political and economic liberation.

[12]Ibid., p. 134. [13]Ibid., p. 122. [14]Ibid., p. 134. [15]Ibid., p. 122.

[16]Ibid., p. 123. [17]Ibid., p. 122. [18]Ibid., p. 125. [19]Ibid., p. 105.

[20]Ibid., p. 106. [21]Ibid., pp. 113-115. [22]Ibid., p. 123. [23]Ibid., p. 116.

[24]Ibid., pp. 123-124. [25]Ibid., p. 124. [26]Ibid., p. 115.

[27]Ibid., p. 117. [28]Ibid.

[29]Quade, *The Pope*, p. 118. A practical problem arises here. How can the Church be at the forefront of socio-political and economic transformation and not intervene directly in politics? If there is only "one universal Church," clergy and laity, advocating justice, is not the Church directly involved in politics? One could answer, in accordance with Vatican II, that it is the responsibility of the laity to run for, and hold, political office. But that is only part of the answer. Vatican II also states that it is the clergy who teach the laity correct political and economic ethics. If this is true, then political and economic responsibility rightly rests with the clergy. And the Church, in its fullness, is directly involved in politics. The standard by which the goals of universal employment and a dynamic, self-critical society are judged is what John Paul calls either "the common good" or "building up society." He posits four steps for serving the common good. The first is the acquisition of a conscience based on "the demands of God's law, of Christ's message about man, and of the ethical dimension of all human enterprise" (ibid., p. 136). The second step is the commitment of oneself to justice, fraternity, and love over against egoism and hatred. The next step is the cooperation of all persons and groups within society for the common good, regardless of the social and economic status of the person or group; *everyone* must participate in the building of a more just society. Finally, serving the common good is a process of conversion from individual sins to an ever new embodiment of human dignity as revealed by Jesus Christ (ibid., pp. 136-137). This writer believes that liberation theologians have recognized this issue for what it is, mere semantics. In other words, they have owned their responsibility and have acted accordingly. But for some, the semantics is what is "law," as the silencing of Leonardo Boff clearly shows. At the least, the Church needs to think through the ramifications of its words.

[30]Ibid., p. 132.   [31]Ibid., p. 121.   [32]Ibid.   [33]Ibid., p. 111.   [34]Ibid.

[35]Ibid., p. 128.   [36]Ibid., p. 135.   [37]Ibid., p. 133.

[38]Sacred Congregation for the Doctrine of the Faith, *Instruction on Certain Aspects of the "Theology of Liberation"* (Boston: Daughters of St. Paul, 1984), cited hereafter as *Instruction on the "Theology of Liberation"* and *Instruction on Christian Freedom and Liberation* (Boston: Daughters of St. Paul, 1986), cited hereafter as *Instruction on Christian Freedom*. For a response to the *Instruction on Certain Aspects of the "Theology of Liberation"*, see Juan Luis Segundo, *Theology and the Church: A Response to Cardinal Ratzinger and a Warning to the Whole Church*, trans. John W. Diercksmeier (Minneapolis: Winston Press, 1985).

[39]Congregation, *Instruction on the "Theology of Liberation"*, Introduction.

[40]Ibid.   [41]Congregation, *Instruction on Christian Freedom*, n. 2.   [42]Ibid.

[43]Congregation, *Instruction on the "Theology of Liberation"*, Introduction.

[44]Ibid., VII, n. 1-11.   [45]Ibid., X, n. 5.   [46]Ibid., IX, n. 4, 5, and 7.

[47]Ibid., X, n. 7.

[48]Ibid., X, n. 11. This writer believes the congregation completely misunderstands liberation Christology. Neither Boff nor Sobrino deny "faith in the Incarnate Word, dead and risen for all." Jesus proclaimed the kingdom of God to both the rich and the poor, women and men, Jew and Gentile. They do not reduce Jesus to the status of a revolutionary symbol. Both men go to great lengths to show that Jesus is "true God and true man." Nor is their portrayal of Jesus' death "an exclusively political event" devoid of spiritual or theological content. Jesus died because he

was faithful to his mission to establish God's kingdom on earth, not because he began a revolution against the Roman Empire.

The congregation rightly interprets liberation Christology's emphasis upon Jesus' partiality for the poor. It is also true that such a stance is revolutionary because it calls into question the political and religious structures that, however unknowingly, sanction oppression. But it does not follow that partiality entails violence. Boff and Sobrino faithfully follow the scriptural witness that Jesus eschewed violence. To be sure, Jesus was involved in many conflicts, but in the end he was the victim of violence rather than its instigator.

[49]Congregation, *Instruction on Christian Freedom*, n. 9, 10, and 12.

[50]Congregation, *Instruction on the "Theology of Liberation"*, IX, n. 13.

[51]Ibid., X, n. 16.

[52]Congregation, *Instruction on Christian Freedom*, n. 20 and 23.

[53]Congregation, *Instruction on the "Theology of Liberation"*, XI, n. 6.   [54]Ibid., n. 8.

[55]Ibid., Introduction. Cf. *Instruction on Christian Freedom*, n. 37-39: Sin is defined as "man's breaking away from God," a denial of one's nature expressed in the desire to be God. In other words, sin is idolatry, a turning from the Creator to the creature.

[56]Congregation, *Instruction on Christian Freedom*, n. 75.

[57]See Congregation, *Instruction on the "Theology of Liberation"*, X, n. 2, 3, 4, and 5. The congregation specifically mentions the documents *Mater et magistra, Pacem in terris, Populorum progressio, Evangelii nuntiandi, Octogesima adveniens, Gaudium et spes, Redemptor hominis, Dives in misericordia, Laborem exercens,* and *Justice and Peace.*

[58]Congregation, *Instruction on the "Theology of Liberation"*, n. 12-16. In *Instruction on Christian Freedom*, the congregation also delineated the roles of the church (n. 80), of a theology of work (n. 82-88), and of culture (n. 92-96) for the transformation of society. They are not covered here because they reiterate John Paul II's position on these subjects above.

[59]Congregation, *Instruction on Christian Freedom*, n. 49. For more detail concerning the congregation's exegesis of the biblical foundation for liberation, see *Instruction on the "Theology of Liberation"*, n. 2-15.

[60]Congregation, *Instruction on Christian Freedom*, n. 68.   [61]Ibid., n. 58-60.

[62]Schubert M. Ogden, *Faith and Freedom: Toward a Theology of Liberation*, revised and enlarged ed. (Nashville: Abingdon Press, 1989), cited hereafter as *Faith*. The reason Christology is chapter four is that Ogden holds that Christology flows from the doctrine of God. Ogden's doctrine of God has two parts: faith, the existential experience of God (chapter two) and the metaphysical being of God (chapter three). The existential meaning of God "that is properly called Christian faith in God is a way of existing and acting *in* freedom and *for* it" (pp. 42-43). Reflection upon this experience leads to the metaphysical, or actual, being of God. If faith is existence in and for freedom, then God, in and of Godself, must be the ground of freedom. God is the ground of freedom as Redeemer, "the one to whom all things make a difference," and as

Emancipator, "the one who makes a difference to all things" (p. 73). As Redeemer, God redeems creation from sin, death, and transcience (p. 71) "for the freedom of faith" (p. 73). As Emancipator, God optimizes the possibilities of the freedom of faith for good while minimizing the possibilities for evil (p. 74). On the basis of this God, Jesus Christ is the "decisive representation of freedom" (p. 93). In other words, the doctrines of God and Christology mutually inform one another, even though the former logically precedes the latter.

63Ogden, *Faith*, p. 93.   64Ibid., pp. 93-95.   65Ibid., p. 95.   66Ibid.

67Ibid., pp. 96-97. To be sure, liberation Christology does not deny that Jesus is the one "through whom" one believes in God. But, equally important, is the assertion that one also believes in God "with" Jesus. Ogden is referring specifically to Jon Sobrino's view of the historical Jesus in *Christology at the Crossroads*.

68Ogden, *Faith*, pp. 98-100. Ogden does give credit where credit is due regarding this mistake. See p. 101: "If the variation on this common pattern worked out by the theologies of liberation is in any way distinctive, it is solely the consistent and thoroughgoing way in which they interpret the existence of faith as the existence of freedom--as the liberated and liberating existence of which Jesus' own existence is taken to be the perfect actualization."

69Ibid., p. 98.   70Ibid., p. 83.   71Ibid., pp. 39-40 and 82-84.   72Ibid., p. 59.

73Ibid., p. 62.   74Ibid., pp. 63-67.   75Ibid., pp. 84-85.

76Ibid., pp. 84-91.   77Ibid., pp. 21-22.   78Ibid., pp. 54-55.

79Ibid., pp. 74-75.   80Ibid., pp. 77-78.   81Ibid., p. 78.   82Ibid., p. 52.

83Ibid., p. 54.

84Orlando E. Costas, a Latin American who taught at Andover Newton, wrote three books which substantively dealt with liberation theology and its Christology. They are: *The Church and its Mission: A Shattering Critique from the Third World* (Wheaton, Ill: Tyndale House Publishing, 1974), pp. 219-64; *Christ Outside the Gate: Mission Beyond Christendom* (Maryknoll: Orbis Books, 1982); and *Liberating News: A Theology of Contextual Evangelization* (Grand Rapids: Eerdmans, 1989).

85For example, Raymond C. Hundley, *Radical Liberation Theology: An Evangelical Response* (Wilmore, KY: Bristol Books, 1987), pp. 2; 23-34. Hundley equated revolution and violence, which he saw as the logical result of liberation theology's use of Marxism which, according to him, had replaced the Bible as the rule of Christian faith. Christology was mentioned substantively only on pp. 39-43; 49-50; 65; and 68-72. See also Carl F. H. Henry, "Insights on Liberation Theology," *United Evangelical Action*, 45 (1986), 5-6, who also equates revolution with violence, thereby rejecting a "revolutionary Jesus" who is the forerunner of Marx and Mao. His criticism rests on the priority of the "lordship of Christ" (which he does not define) which is independent of any political liberation. A different approach is found in C. Peter Wagner, *Latin American Theology: Radical or Evangelical?: The Struggle for the Faith of a Young Church* (Grand Rapids: Eerdmans, 1970), pp. 21-109. Wagner implied a criticism of liberation Christology from the perspective of an Evangelical ecclesiology that has personal soul-winning as its primary purpose. Of these representative examples, only Hundley referred to any christological writings, Boff's *Jesus Christ Liberator*. Even then, he did not see it as being critical of Marxism. This situation can only be interpreted as either a benign ignorance of liberation Christology or as a deliberate oversight because liberation Christology did not fit their ideological critique.

86Clark H. Pinnock, "An Evangelical Theology of Human Liberation," *Sojourners*, 5 (1976), 30. Cited hereafter as "Part 1."

87Ibid.   88Ibid., 31.

89Clark H. Pinnock, "An Evangelical Theology of Human Liberation: Part 2," *Sojourners*, 5 (1976), 26. Cited hereafter as "Part 2."

90Pinnock, "Part 1," 33.   91Ibid., 32.   92Ibid., 31.

93Pinnock probably would not use this terminology today. Cf. Clark H. Pinnock, "A Pilgrimage in Political Theology--A Personal Witness," in *Liberation Theology*, ed. Ronald Nash (Milford, Michigan: Mott Media, 1984), pp. 111-17, where he renounces his "radical" evangelicalism of 1970-78. Cited hereafter as "Pilgrimage."

94Pinnock, "Part 1," 31.   95Pinnock, "Part 2," 27.

96Ibid., 26. It is doubtful that Pinnock senses the same urgency today that he felt in 1976. Cf. Pinnock, "Pilgrimage," p. 111: "Late in the 1970s. . . . I began . . . to see once again the positive tendencies of democratic capitalism which had been eclipsed" [in his radical period]. He goes on to say: "In the case of our Western democracies, it seems plain to me now that the Christian heritage operating in them is profound and precious, and renders them worthy of critical support and reforming efforts" (p. 114).

97Pinnock, "Part 2," 28.   98Ibid.   99Ibid.   100Ibid.   101Ibid.   102Ibid., 29.

103Ibid.   104Pinnock, "Part 1," 33.   105Ibid., 32.   106Ibid.   107Ibid., 32.

108Ibid., 33.   109Pinnock, "Part 2," 29.

110See above, pp. 242-243. This is the point where Pinnock has changed the most. Marxist societies are those "where neither liberty nor justice is in good supply" ("Pilgrimage," p. 112). Marxism "answers to no transcendent value" and is "the destruction of the human spirit" (ibid.). "Socialism," he said, "has a dismal record of providing [liberty and prosperity]" (ibid., p. 114).
111Cf. n. 48 above.

112Boff had an opportunity to explore this possibility in his book, *Trinity and Society*, trans. Paul Burns (Maryknoll: Orbis Books, 1988), but did not do so. To this writer's knowledge, process theology has not been a dialogue partner for liberation theology.

APPENDIX

Boff's criticism of Moltmann should not be taken lightly. Moltmann goes to great lengths, using very clear language, to show that the Father willed the death of the Son; that God abandoned Jesus on the cross and left him to die. Such a view provides a rather treacherous road for a loving God to travel. If God did this to Jesus, what prohibits God from doing the same to anyone else who strives to follow God in this world? Moltmann's reply would be that in dying a God-forsaken death, Jesus insured that no one else must die alone. While this is of some comfort, it does little to eliminate the nagging thought that one still might die abandoned by the God one is attempting to follow.

This dialogue reveals two major differences between the Christology of Boff and that of Moltmann. Traditionally stated, the first difference is the interpretation of the Person and Work of Christ. Boff emphasizes the former. His Franciscan heritage stresses the humanity of Jesus. He lived his life as would any other human being: in faith and freedom before God, not knowing beforehand the outcome of any given action but trusting God throughout. This presentation of Jesus parallels Boff's view of the predicament of Latin American Christians. They are called to a lifestyle that conflicts with the status quo, believing that God will accept them no matter what the outcome. Thus, Boff's Christology serves as an ethic of discipleship.

Moltmann's Reformed heritage places him on the other side of the coin. His emphasis is upon the divinity of Christ. Jesus, the Son of God, was playing his part in the drama of salvation as "the Lamb of God slain before the foundation of the world." This presentation of Jesus provides the answers to the questions Moltmann sees plaguing Western (European) society. Jesus' godforsaken death breaks the death-dealing grip of meaninglessness, nihilism, and atheism. Thus, Moltmann's Christology serves as an explication of the salvation wrought by Christ.

The second difference follows closely upon the first. A basic tenet of liberation theology is that one's *Sitz im Leben* profoundly impacts how one experiences God and talks about that experience. On the one hand, Boff is writing from the Latin American experience of colonialism and underdevelopment, a situation that cries out for a God who liberates from oppression. In a very practical sense, the people have no power to change their own situation. They hope that living out their faith in Christ will effect a change in the structures governing their life. Moltmann, on the other hand, is writing from a position of power. The people he addresses have the power to change their lot in life. They can change jobs, further their education, and decide between political candidates. What they need is the knowledge to help them make those changes, that is, knowledge of their problems, and of the possible solutions.

These differences are not devastating critiques of either Moltmann's Christology or of Boff's. They do, however, point out that both Christologies are situation-oriented, and that both are necessary to meet the needs of the people in two very different cultural situations. For the ways these Christologies may complement each other, see Jürgen Moltmann, "The Liberation of Oppressors," *Journal of Theology for Southern Africa*, 26 (1979), 24-37.

BIBLIOGRAPHY

Abbott, Walter M., gen. ed. *The Documents of Vatican II: All Sixteen Official Texts Promulgated by the Ecumenical Council 1963-1965.* New York: Herder and Herder, 1966.

Berryman, Phillip. *Liberation Theology: Essential Facts about the Revolutionary Movement in Latin America and Beyond.* Oak Park, IL: Meyer Stone Books, 1987.

_____. *The Religious Roots of Rebellion: Christians in Central American Revolutions.* Maryknoll: Orbis Books, 1984.

Boff, Leonardo. *Church: Charism and Power: Liberation Theology and the Institutional Church.* Trans. John W. Diercksmeier. New York: Crossroad, 1986.

_____. *Ecclesiogenesis: The Base Communities Reinvent the Church.* Trans. Robert R. Barr. Maryknoll: Orbis Books, 1986.

_____. *O Evangelho do Cristo Cósmico: A Realidade de um Mito, O Mito de uma Realidade.* Petrópolis, RJ: Editôra Vozes Ltda, 1971.

_____. *Jesus Christ Liberator: A Critical Christology for Our Time.* Trans. Patrick Hughes. Maryknoll: Orbis Books, 1978.

_____. *Liberating Grace.* Trans. John Drury. Maryknoll: Orbis Books, 1979.

_____. *Passion of Christ, Passion of the World: The Facts, Their Interpretation, and Their Meaning Yesterday and Today.* Trans. Robert R. Barr. Maryknoll: Orbis Books, 1987.

_____. *The Question of Faith in the Resurrection of Jesus.* Trans. Luis Runde. Chicago, Ill: Franciscan Herald Press, 1971.

_____. *A Ressurreição da Cristo: A nossa Ressurreicao no Morte.* 3d ed. Petrópolis, RJ: Editôra Vozes Ltda, 1971.

_____. *Sacraments of Life, Life of the Sacraments.* Trans. John Drury. Washington, D. C.: The Pastoral Press, 1987.

_____. *Trinity and Society.* Trans. Paul Burns. Maryknoll: Orbis Books, 1988.

_____. *Way of the Cross--Way of Justice.* Trans. John Drury. Maryknoll: Orbis Books, 1980.

Boff, Leonardo and Clodovis Boff. *Liberation Theology: From Dialogue to Confrontation.* Trans. Robert R. Barr. San Francisco: Harper & Row, 1986.

Cardenal, Ernesto. *The Gospel According to Solentiname*, 4 vols. Trans. and rev. Alan Neely. Maryknoll: Orbis Books, 1976-1982.

CELAM. *The Church in the Present-Day Transformation of Latin America in the Light of the Council*, Vol. II, 3d ed. National Conference of Catholic Bishops: Washington, D.C., 1979.

Costas, Orlando E. *Christ Outside the Gate: Mission Beyond Christendom.* Maryknoll: Orbis Books, 1982.

_____. *The Church and its Mission: A Shattering Critique from the Third World.* Wheaton, Ill: Tyndale House Publishing, 1974.

_____. *Liberating News: A Theology of Contextual Evangelization.* Grand Rapids: Eerdmans, 1989.

Dussell, Enrique. *History of the Church in Latin America: Colonialism to Liberation.* Trans. Donald D. Walsh. Grand Rapids: William B. Eerdmans Publishing Company, 1981.

Ferm, Deane William. *Profiles in Liberation: 36 Portraits of Third World Theologians.* Mystic, Connecticut: Twenty-Third Publications, 1988.

_____. *Third World Liberation Theologies: An Introductory Survey.* Maryknoll: Orbis Books, 1986.

Gutiérrez, Gustavo. *A Theology of Liberation: History, Politics and Salvation*, rev. ed. Trans. and ed. Sr. Caridad Inda and John Eagleson. Maryknoll: Orbis Books, 1988.

_____. *We Drink from Our Own Wells: The Spiritual Journey of a People.* Trans. Matthew J. O'Connell. Maryknoll: Orbis Books, 1984.

Henry, Carl F. H. "Insights on Liberation Theology." *United Evangelical Action*, 45 (1986), 5-6.

Hundley, Raymond C. *Radical Liberaiton Theology: An Evangelical Response.* Wilmore, KY: Bristol Books, 1987.

Luis Segundo, Juan. *The Liberation of Theology.* Trans. John Drury. Maryknoll: Orbis Books, 1976.

_____. *Theology and the Church: A Response to Cardinal Ratzinger and a Warning to the Whole Church.* Trans. John W. Diercksmeier. Minneapolis: Winston Press, 1985.

Mackay, John A. *The Other Spanish Christ: A Study of the Spiritual History of Spain and South America.* New York: Macmillan, 1932.

Míguez Bonino, José. *Doing Theology in a Revolutionary Situation.* Philadelphia: Fortress Press, 1975.

Moltmann, Jürgen. "Christian Theology and Political Religion." *Civil Religion and Political Theology.* Ed. Leroy S. Rouner. Notre Dame: University of Notre Dame Press, 1986.

Moltmann, Jürgen. "The Christian Theology of Hope and Its Bearing on Development." *In Search of a Theology of Development: Papers from a Consultation on Theology and Development Held by SODEPAX in Cartigny, Switzerland, November, 1969*. Lausanne: Imprimerie La Concorde, ND.

_____. *The Church in the Power of the Spirit: A Contribution to Messianic Ecclesiology*. Trans. Margaret Kohl. New York: Harper and Row, 1977.

_____. *The Crucified God: The Cross of Christ as the Foundation and Criticism of Christian Theology*. Trans. R. A. Wilson and John Bowden. New York: Harper and Row, 1974.

_____. *God in Creation: A New Theology of Creation and the Spirit of God: The Gifford Lectures 1984-1985*. Trans. Margaret Kohl. New York: Harper and Row, 1985.

_____. "God's Kingdom as the Meaning of Life and of the World." Trans. Theo Weston. *Why Did God Make Me?* Eds. Hans Küng and Jürgen Moltmann. New York: Seabury Press, 1978.

_____. "The Inviting Unity of the Triune God." Trans. Robert Nowell. *Monotheism*. Eds. Claude Geffré and Jean-Pierre Jossua. Edinburgh: T and T Clark, 1985

_____. "The Liberating Feast." Trans. Francis McDonagh. *Politics and Liturgy*. Eds. Herman Schmidt and David Power. New York: Herder and Herder, 1974.

_____. "The Liberation of Oppressors." *Journal of Theology for Southern Africa*, 26 (1979), 24-37.

_____. "Theology of Mystical Experience." *Scottish Journal of Theology*, 32 (1979), 513-17.

_____. *The Trinity and the Kingdom: The Doctrine of God*. Trans. Margaret Kohl. New York: Harper and Row, 1981.

Ogden, Schubert M. *Faith and Freedom: Toward a Theology of Liberation*, rev. and enlarged ed. Nashville: Abingdom Press, 1989.

Ostling, Richard A. "A Lesson on Liberation." *Time*, April 14, 1986, p. 84.

Pannenberg, Wolfhart. *Anthropology in Theological Perspective*. Trans. Matthew J. O'Connell. Philadelphia: Westminster Press, 1985.

_____. *The Apostles' Creed in the Light of Today's Questions*. Trans. Margaret Kohl. Philadelphia: Westminster, 1972.

_____. *Basic Questions in Theology: Collected Essays*, Vol. I. Trans. George H. Kehn. Philadelphia: Fortress Press, 1970.

_____. *Christian Spirituality*. Philadelphia: Westminster Press, 1983.

134

Pannenberg, Wolfhart. "Christianity, Marxism, and Liberation Theology." *Christian Scholars Review*, 18 (1989), 215-26.

_____. "Constructive and Critical Functions of Christian Eschatology." *Harvard Theological Review*, 27 (1984), 123-25.

_____. "God's Presence in History." *The Christian Century*, March 11, 1981, p. 263.

_____. *Jesus--God and Man*. 2nd ed. Trans. Lewis L. Wilkins and Duane A. Priebe. Philadelphia: Westminster Press, 1968.

_____. "The Resurrection of Jesus and the Future of Mankind." Trans. M. B. Jackson. *The Cumberland Seminarian*, XIX (1981), 44-45.

_____. *Theology and the Kingdom of God*. Trans. Richard John Neuhaus. Philadelphia: Westminster Press, 1969.

_____. "A Theology of the Cross." *Word and World*, VIII (1988), 167.

Pannenberg, Wolfhart, et al. *Revelation as History*. Trans. David Granskou. New York: The Macmillan Company, 1968.

Pinnock, Clark H. "An Evangelical Theology of Human Liberation." *Sojourners*, 5 (1976), 30-33.

_____. "An Evangelical Theology of Human Liberation: Part 2." *Sojourners*, 5 (1976), 26-29.

_____. "A Pilgrimmage in Political Theology." *Liberation Theology*. Ed. Ronald Nash. Milford, Michigan: Mott Media, 1984.

Quade, Quentin L., ed. *The Pope and Revolution: John Paul II Confronts Liberation Theology*. Washington, D.C.: Ethics and Public Policy Center, 1982.

Rahner, Karl. "Anonymous Christians." *Theological Investigations*, Vol. VI. Trans. Karl-H. and Boniface Kruger. Baltimore: Helicon Press, 1969.

_____. "Atheism and Implicit Christianity." *Theological Investigations*, Vol. IX. Trans. Graham Harrison. London: Darton, Longman and Todd, 1972.

Sacred Congregation for the Doctrine of the Faith. *Instruction on Certain Aspects of the "Theology of Liberation"*. Boston: Daughters of St. Paul, 1984.

_____. *Instruction on Christian Freedom and Liberation*. Boston: Daughters of St. Paul, 1986.

Schillebeeckx, Edward. *Jesus: An Experiment in Christology*. Trans. Herbert Hoskins. New York: Crossroad, 1981.

Schoonenberg, Piet. *The Christ: A Study of the God-Man Relationship in the Whole of Creation and in Jesus Christ.* Trans. Della Couling. New York: Herder and Herder, 1971.

Severino Croatto, J. *Exodus: A Hermeneutic of Freedom.* Trans. Salvator Attanasio. Maryknoll: Orbis Books, 1981.

Simpson, Gary M. "Whither Wolfhart Pannenberg? Reciprocity and Political Theology." *The Journal of Religion*, 67 (1987), 33-49.

Sobrino, Jon. *Christology at the Crossroads: A Latin American Approach.* Trans. John Drury. Maryknoll: Orbis Books, 1978.

_____. "Current Problems in Christology in Latin America Today." Trans. Fernando Segovia. *Theology and Discovery: Essays in Honor of Karl Rahner, S.J.* Ed. William J. Kelly. Milwaukee, Wisconsin: Marquette University Press, 1980.

_____. *Jesus in Latin America.* Maryknoll: Orbis Books, 1987.

_____. *Resurrección de la Verdadera Iglesia: Los Pobres,lugar teológico de la eclesiología*, 2nd ed. Santander, Spain: Editorial Sal Terre, 1984.

_____. *Romero: Martyr for Liberation.* London: Catholic Institute for International Relations, 1982.

_____. *Spirituality of Liberation: Toward Political Holiness.* Trans. Robert R. Barr. Maryknoll: Orbis Books, 1988.

_____. *The True Church and the Poor.* Trans. Matthew J. O'Connell. Maryknoll: Orbis Books, 1984.

_____. "The Witness of the Church in Latin America." *The Challenge of Basic Christian Communities: Papers from the International Ecumenical Congress of Theology, February 20-March 2, 1980, Sao Paulo, Brazil.* Eds. Sergio Torres and John Eagleson. Trans. John Drury. Maryknoll: Orbis Books, 1981.

Sobrino, Jon and Juan Hernandez Pico. *Theology of Christian Solidarity.* Trans. Philip Berryman. Maryknoll: Orbis Books, 1985.

Wagner, C. Peter. *Latin American Theology: Radical or Evangelical?: The Struggle for the Faith in a Young Church.* Grand Rapids: Eerdmans, 1970.

Williamson, Clark M. "Christ Against the Jews: A Review of Jon Sobrino's Christology." *Encounter*, 40 (1979), 410.

VITA

Donald E. Waltermire

PERSONAL
  Born: November 15, 1957; Lexington, Kentucky
  Parents: Donald Eugene and Betty Stone Waltermire

EDUCATIONAL
  Public Schools, Lexington, Kentucky, 1963-1975
  B.A., Campbellsville College, 1980
  M.Div., The Southern Baptist Theological Seminary, December 1983
  Ph. D., The Southern Baptist Theological Seminary, May 1990

MINISTERIAL
  Co-Minister of Youth, Boone's Creek Baptist Church, Lexington, Kentucky,
    Summer 1975
  Son Share Players, Kentucky Baptist Student Union, Summer 1979
  Minister to Youth and Children, Bellfield Baptist Church, Henderson,
    Kentucky, Summer 1979
  Summer Missionary, Kentucky Baptist Convention, First Baptist Church,
    Wheelwright, Kentucky 1982
  Minister to Senior Adults, Immanuel Baptist Church, Louisville, Kentucky,
    1982-1983
  Associate Pastor, Immanuel Baptist Church, Louisville, Kentucky, 1983-1986
  Coordinator of Social Services, St. John Center, Inc., Louisville, Kentucky,
    1987-Present

ACADEMIC
  Garrett Fellow, Historical-Theological Department, Spring 1985
  Who's Who in Religion, 1992-1993

DATE DUE